D0381242

# Your Spiritual Director

# Jesus Our Spiritual Director

## A PILGRIMAGE THROUGH THE GOSPELS

## WENDY J. MILLER

UPPER ROOM BOOKS®
NASHVILLE

**Jesus, Our Spiritual Director**
*A Pilgrimage through the Gospels*
© 2004 by Wendy J. Miller
All rights reserved.

No part of this book may be reproduced in any manner whatsoever without written permission of the publisher except in brief quotations in critical articles or reviews. For information, write Upper Room Books, 1908 Grand Avenue, Nashville, Tennessee 37212.

The Upper Room® Web site: www.upperroom.org

UPPER ROOM®, UPPER ROOM BOOKS®, and design logos are trademarks owned by The Upper Room®, Nashville, Tennessee. All rights reserved.

Unless otherwise noted, scripture quotations are from the New Revised Standard Version Bible, copyright 1989 Division of Christian Education of the National Council of the Churches of Christ in the United States of America. Used by permission. All rights reserved.

Scripture quotations marked (NIV) are taken from the HOLY BIBLE, NEW INTERNATIONAL VERSION. NIV. Copyright 1973, 1978, 1984 by International Bible Society. Used by permission of Zondervan Publishing House. All rights reserved.

Scripture noted AP is the author's paraphrase.

Diagram on page 25 is from *The Spiritual Director: A Practical Guide* by Damien Isabell. Copyright © 1976 by Franciscan Herald Press. Used by permission of Franciscan Press.

Retreat session plans on pages 121 ff. may be photocopied with inclusion of the copyright notice that appears on this page.

Cover and interior design: TMW Designs
Interior implementation: Nancy Cole-Hatcher
Cover image: SuperStock
First printing: 2004

Library of Congress Cataloging-in-Publication Data
Miller, Wendy.
    Jesus, our spiritual director : a pilgrimage through the Gospels / by Wendy J. Miller.
    p. cm.
Includes bibliographical references.
    ISBN 0-8358-9876-8
  1. Spiritual direction. 2. Spiritual life—Christianity. 3. Bible. N.T. Gospels—Devotional use.    I. Title.
    BV5053.M54  2004
    253.5'3—dc22                  2003019488
Printed in the United States of America

I write this work companioned by the memory of

### Hans Schlaffer

a follower of Jesus who was imprisoned in Schwatz,
Austria, and died for his faith in February 1528.
He was an Anabaptist who lived and prayed into
the meaning and practice of the gospel during the
tumultuous years of the Reformation.
As Hans prayed his way through those days before his death,
he experienced the help and companionship of Jesus
whom he came to know as

### *"shepherd, door of the sheep barn, . . .*
### *our reconciler, mediator, spiritual guide and pastor."* *

* From words spoken in prayer by Hans Schlaffer at Schwatz, Austria, shortly before his death. *Spiritual Life in Anabaptism*, ed. Cornelius J. Dyck (Scottdale, Pa.: Herald Press, 1995), 202.

# CONTENTS

# INTRODUCTION

$W$ithin the past decade new words have made their way into our language in the church, terms such as *spiritual disciplines, spiritual formation,* and *spiritual direction.* Although familiar in the early Christian tradition, these ancient terms for soul care are still fairly new to us. New books on prayer and spiritual direction are also appearing on our bookshelves. Within this ancient tradition of soul care, persons offering spiritual guidance point to God as *the* Director and often include references to both the Hebrew and New Testament scriptures in their writings. However, very little has been written about how Jesus serves as spiritual guide within the Gospels.

In these colorful gospel narratives we can discover Jesus offering soul care to men and women, youth and children, to crowds, to small groups, to families, and to individuals. In order to enter into this experience more fully, I employ the more recent narrative approach to studying the Gospels. Using this approach, "one temporarily takes leave of one's familiar world of reality and enters into another world. . . . By inhabiting this world one experiences it, and having experienced it, one leaves and returns, perhaps changed, to one's own world."[1] I also draw on ancient voices from the early centuries of the church who together point to the apostle Simon Peter as the voice behind Mark's gospel narrative.[2] Simon Peter will serve as one of our hosts and guides for this pilgrimage into the world of Mark's Gospel. Other disciples and those who listened closely to their storied experience—Matthew, John, and finally Luke—also will companion us.

With gracious hospitality the disciples invite us into the rhythm of their life and activity together. We join them in communal and private conversation, in active ministry, and in times of solitude and retreat. The spiritual discipline of entering the biblical narrative will assist us in this pilgrimage of the soul (see chapter 3).

These early followers of Jesus reveal how human and limited they are in their understanding of who Jesus is; how slow to read the map he offers, and how dependent they are on Jesus and the Spirit of God to help them recognize and know the Christ. We become privy to their questions, their problems, their resistances, their gradual growth in faith. Their worldview, embedded within their storied experience, contains preunderstandings of Jesus as the Messiah that block their understanding of what his life and work is really about. Today we are as slow to recognize and read the map Jesus offers as the disciples were.

Thus we receive in the Gospels a pastoral paradigm: It is difficult for persons to move past preunderstandings within their tradition and story—whether in the time of Jesus or in our present age; and, learning and transformation occur slowly. Just as Jesus offered pastoral care and guidance to his followers in this process of map reading, learning, and change, he also becomes our pastoral and spiritual guide. Jesus models for us how to do the work of ministry—what to notice, what to embrace, what to let go of, how to respond. Jesus becomes our map and the map-maker for ministry.

I wrote this book with pastors, church leaders, Sunday school teachers, small-group leaders, youth sponsors, elders, deacons, and other servants of God in mind: those of us who minister to persons in the midst of their life experience. As we listen to women and men, youth and young adults, and even to children, we hear how driven, busy, tired, and well-meaning each person is. One office worker was heard saying, "I can only afford to take my two weeks' vacation over a weekend. I don't have money or time for anything else." People work hard to pay bills, to succeed, to somehow manage all that needs to be taken care of in life, but they often see their goals (and their income) disappear in the shifting sands of world-wide complexity and change. As pastors and servants of God we are also aware of loss of place and voice. We wonder about our role in this age when persons seek out medical doctors and psychologists for authoritative guidance and turn to the Internet for information rather than to the church for guidance. Our identity and a firm sense of pastoral ministry's purpose seem to be in question as we seek a way through this fragmented, fast-moving, and bewildering age.

Within and beyond the church, however, persons are searching for meaning, desiring to find a frame of reference in a world where the center no longer seems to hold. The widespread interest in many forms of spirituality signals a deep-felt hunger and search for something more than the material. A growing number of persons in and beyond the church are reading classical works on spirituality and books on spiritual guidance, many of which have been overlooked for centuries by Christian scholars and persons in ministry. In this postmodern wilderness where many lack security or a center that provides direction and meaning, persons seek streams for their spirits and bread for their souls. There are signs of hope and of God's presence and work in the world. However, as pastors and servants of God, we are not always sure how to respond to persons engaged in this search.

David had been a pastor for over thirty years. Well-liked and respected in the growing congregation in which he serves, he had learned to perform administrative tasks with ease. Seminary had prepared him well for this; so also the various seminars he had attended over the years. He sensed something missing in his own life and ministry. As he sat with a small group of pastors who felt a similar dis-ease, he said, "The CEO model for pastor seems to work well—at least on the surface—but this approach to ministry gets us off track. We're avoiding something central to ministry. I desire to see God at the center. I want to stop running the church and learn how to be a pastor to the people." David decided he needed to learn how to attend to soul care and pay attention to encouraging spiritual formation within the congregation.

David is not alone. More and more pastors, youth leaders, and persons who serve in the church request guidance for offering soul care. They are searching for ways to attend to spiritual formation in the congregation and for help in ministering to persons who seek spiritual direction. I am reminded of Thomas and the early disciples as their expectations concerning the Messiah were shifting and collapsing. This Jesus to whom they looked as the Messiah was about to leave them and return to God. They had expected God to send them a messiah who would be king, restore the political fortunes and throne to the people of Israel, and free them from Roman occupation and rule. Now Jesus was about to leave. What would they do? What was God up to? "How can we know the way?" Thomas asks—for himself and for all those present. Jesus responds simply, "I am the way, and the truth, and the life." With this answer Jesus places himself at front and center, a radical alternative to their programmatic messianic expectations. Thus Jesus offers guidance as they seek a way to live, seek reality and truth, and search for a life worth living in the light of God's way. In time these early disciples grasp the truth of who Jesus is. And they in turn give us a map, directing our attention to Jesus and the good news of God's gracious rule.

## How to Use This Book

In the first three chapters, I invite you on a tour of the contemporary context in which we live and offer soul care, paying attention to what we mean by the term *spiritual direction*. Our journey includes tracing some of the history that shapes the map imbedded in our personal and collective stories. We will also pay attention to the way in which we can find all our stories and their meaning within the Great Story of God in Christ. In chapter 3 we will learn how to recognize and read the invitations offered by the early gospel writers to enter the world of the gospel narrative.

Beginning in chapter 4, the gospel narrators guide us as we begin a pilgrimage into the Gospels. They invite us to come alongside, to be present with Jesus' followers, to hear Jesus' invitation to be with him, and then to be sent out to preach the good news of the kingdom (Mark 3:13-15). They invite us to listen in to the experiences, responses, and resistance toward the new thing God is doing in Jesus. Simon Peter, through the narratives collected and penned by Mark, will serve as our primary guide. However, as other men and women enter into the story, they will also be serving as our companions on the way.

## FORMATIVE READING AND ENGAGING WITH THE TEXT

We have been schooled in reading for information and usually are able to do a quick overview of a text, even biblical text or spiritual reading. *Formative* reading happens when we read slowly, not seeking to control, outline, or analyze the content. Here we are invited to come as listeners, receptive to the content and alert to the presence of the Spirit of God within and behind scripture. Then the gospel narrative begins to read us and shape us, assisting us to see and to read the map being offered. With the intent of the gospel writers in mind, this book is designed to invite such encounter, so each chapter contains the following elements.

### MATERIAL FOR PERSONAL READING

In the first three chapters, the content gives background and information to orient and prepare for our journey into the narrative of the Gospels. Starting with chapter 4 and following, the chapter content moves in concert with the gospel narrative. Scripture references are given from Mark's Gospel, along with parallel passages from other Gospels and an invitation for prayerful reading of the scripture.

The Gospels also record a number of dialogues Jesus had with individual women and men. Several "Dialogues with Jesus," such conversations arranged like transcripts, are available on the Web at www. upperroom.org/dialogues. I will refer to these in the book.

### INVITATIONS TO REFLECTION

Each chapter includes several pauses that offer guidance for reflection and journaling as you read. Some "Reflection" sections include guidance for practice of spiritual disciplines.

### ATTENDING TO SPIRITUAL GUIDANCE

In each chapter, the section "Attending to Spiritual Guidance" outlines the pastoral practice and ministry of companioning others on their spiritual journey. As an individual reader, you are invited to gather with other servants of God who are also reading and engaging with the text. Structure and guidance will be given for a group leader and group members to move through these activities:

- Gathering and forming a group covenant
- Practicing a guided meditation
- Discernment following meditation
- Group work and reflection in group and in one-on-one conversations attending to soul care, spiritual direction.

Text in bold type provides a script the leader may use or adapt in moving the group through each session.

Ideally such a group meeting will last two hours, giving time for learning, discussion, and experiential practice in giving spiritual guidance. If two hours are not available, you may adapt the way you work with this section, possibly planning two sessions instead of one to cover the material.

## SPENDING A DAY IN RETREAT

I encourage you to spend a day in retreat. Here you will enter into a longer time of rest, prayerful solitude, and soul care. Chapter 8 draws attention to the need for time apart in the rhythm of life and ministry of God's servants.

You will find it helpful to think and plan ahead along with the other members of your group concerning a day and place for the retreat. Be sure to reserve the space you need. Other details you will need to attend to are given at the end of chapter 8. You may wish to invite someone from outside the group to lead this day for you. If so, make plans to invite the person of your choice and give them a copy of this book as he or she prepares to lead.

---

I am especially grateful to John Koenig, professor of New Testament at General Theological Seminary, whose teaching and personal encouragement became a well of courage as I began this work and as I continued to write. My thanks also to Eastern Mennonite University for the generous gift of sabbatical time for reading, reflection, and writing; also for helpful comments and suggestions from students at Eastern Mennonite

Seminary and other persons who read and worked with the manuscript. I thank Lorie Hershey for technical and research assistance; she worked with such expertise and grace. I am grateful to my editors at Upper Room Books, JoAnn Miller and Jeannie Crawford-Lee; they sat with me at the potter's wheel of revision to help me reshape and form this work.

As I work on final revisions for this manuscript, reports of war and the aftermath of war dominate the news. Even as we give thanks for efforts to restore water, electricity, and health care as well as for each individual who can return home—whether in Iraq or elsewhere—we perceive that peace is fragile and soon shattered. We now live in solidarity with millions of persons in the world whose life stories speak of war, loss of family, destruction, and ongoing acts of terror. Thus we also live in solidarity with the early disciples, for such was the social and political climate at the time of Jesus. It is at such a time as this that God sends his Son, the Prince of Peace, into the world.

As you enter this pilgrimage into the gospel narratives, may the wellsprings of the Spirit refresh and restore you along the way. And may the companioning of the Holy Spirit through these early disciples guide your path home to the One who comes to meet and embrace us in Jesus, even as we—like the prodigal son—come to our senses, turn toward home, and discover the peace that the world cannot give.

WENDY J MILLER
*In Easter season, 2003*

Chapter 1

# Seeking Direction

*Blessed are those who hunger and thirst for righteousness,*
*for they will be filled.—Matthew 5:6*

A cold winter chill seeped into the long hours after midnight. I discovered I was not the only one awake. A friendly and rhythmic honking sounded in the night. First distant, then closer, then directly over our Virginia-style metal roof the nocturnal conversation moved: voices of Canadian geese signaling to each other as the geese navigated their way in the dark around the giant maple tree with its branches spread high over our front porch. Gradually these night travelers flew off toward the north, their wings beating in rhythm with a God-made-but-hidden homing instinct, their honking a kind of companioning, one bird signaling direction to another on the long flight home.

I remembered other flights of Canada geese I had watched and heard when we lived in Bethlehem, Pennsylvania. The grassy banks of the river behind our town house served as favorite resting places for these continental travelers flying south in the fall and north as winter slowly gave

way to the overtures of spring. Rather than glide in for a welcome landing, however, the incoming flock shifted into a circling pattern, honking
loudly high above the traffic, the rumble of trains, conversation, and com-
merce in the city. This holding pattern continued until another flock of
geese came into sight and received its signals as to where to land for rest,
food, and water. Only then would the group that was circling descend
smoothly onto the surface of the river, leaving the incoming travelers to
take over the task of giving direction for other geese in flight and in need
of rest and refreshment on their way.

This God-given-but-hidden yearning for home is imbedded deep
within our being. Signs of its presence appear during Thanksgiving,
Christmas, and New Year's holidays when hundreds of thousands of people leave warm and comfortable dwelling places to travel, standing in
long lines at airport counters, driving four lanes abreast in snow and ice
on interstate highways, sitting and waiting on long benches in drafty bus
and train depots, all in some way going "home for the holidays." Each
fall young people leave home for college, but they go equipped for
this annual migration with calling cards and cell phones to help them
stay in touch with loved ones. We see this need for home even more
poignantly in the distant gaze of women, men, and children thrust out
of their houses, villages, and cities as a result of famine, floods, earthquakes, or political upheaval and war. They long to return home, no matter how long the journey.

These journeys point to other journeys we make, journeys of the
soul. Margaret Guenther observes that ever since our expulsion from
Eden—that first home for humankind—we have become "people on the
move, despite attempts at self-delusion that we have somehow arrived."[1]
Although God companions us, we no longer recognize the honkings God
gives; nor do we see the circling patterns God provides, guiding us to
safe landing. Our homing instinct is deaf and blind to the graced signals
of God's presence. One ministry of the church is to help us "ready ourselves for grace, help us to spy it, to take it when it comes."[2] Of course,
we can blame the church for not helping us with this task
of noticing, and our criticism has its grounds. Ben Campbell Johnson,

former pastor and now professor of evangelism and church growth at Columbia Theological Seminary, acknowledges that many who seek out a pastor or priest to talk about their soul will discover that "the minister tries to psychoanalyze them, makes a joke, or changes the subject." Thus "they eventually decide they can't talk to the minister about the things of faith that really matter."[3]

At the same time, if we are truly honest, those of us in the pews also resist God and God's invitations. As a young teenager I began praying for help for our family; we were in need of a place to live. When my prayers were not answered within several weeks, I was convinced that God was not listening. Unknown to me, God was already answering my prayers, even before I began praying. A realtor had found a small house and thought of our family needs. But when God began to invite my attention toward a deeper sense of coming home, I rebelled. I told God I was not interested in Jesus or coming closer to God. I wanted other things more. I resisted and turned a deaf ear to God for the time being.

## REFLECTION

Pause and reflect on your own soul journey.

- In what ways are you aware of God's invitation to "come home," to turn toward God in your life?
- How have you resisted?
- How have you responded?

When people call on the phone or come to my office requesting spiritual direction, I am aware that the God-given-but-hidden homing tug upon the soul is pushing its way from deep within the person and is being given voice, no matter how varied the "honkings"![4]

A university professor calls. "B. gave me your name and phone number. I'm looking for a spiritual director. Is someone available?" Hilda goes on to tell me that she is fifty-two years of age and has been teaching for twenty years. "For most of my life I have been questioning any ideas about having faith in God or believing in spiritual things. But somehow I'm sensing that I need something or someone in whom to anchor my life. That's why I'm calling."

Then there is Jack. "Could I come and talk? My coworker says I need a spiritual director. . . . I don't know how to connect with God. The Bible is just flat words on a flat page for me, and I've never really related to Jesus. But I see how some of the people I work with are having a true and life-changing experience of Jesus. Something in me wants that." Jack is a social worker who assists needy families from various ethnic and cultural backgrounds.

Bob is a pastor. He told me he had lost most of his joy and vision for ministry. "I'm not sure how long I will stay in this new position, maybe a year or two. Maybe it's the experience I had while pastoring another church. It was difficult, painful. And maybe it's because I work too hard; there's always more to do in the church than I can keep up with. I guess I'm always on the run. I put on a good front, but inside I feel kind of lost and lacking in joy. I'm wondering what happened to my sense of call and where God is for me. I heard that spiritual direction could be helpful."

Mim is a seminary student in her mid-thirties. She asks for spiritual direction and then explains why. "God is such an ogre for me," she says frankly. "I'm not sure why I would want to connect with God when I know he will not approve of me if I come close. So I stand at a safe distance. But something in me wants to go closer . . ." She pauses, and I sense she is in deep thought. Then she reflects, "Come to think of it, it's kind of ironic that I'm in seminary, thinking about doing ministry. After all, ministry is about God, isn't it?"

Dan asks if spiritual direction could be helpful for him. A minister, married and the father of three grown children, Dan tells me that his prayer experience is changing. "I'm not sure what it's all about," he says, then pauses for a while. "You will probably think this is weird or something . . ." Another pause. "But when I pray I have begun seeing light. Something seems to lift my attention up to this light. Is spiritual direction the kind of place you talk about this kind of thing?"

Already in these introductory conversations with persons who are inquiring about receiving some spiritual guidance, brief pieces of story are being offered. Like small windows, they shed light on personal history and explain what has brought these people to a place in their experience where they sense a need for God. Most of the time, however, people are not sure what spiritual direction and spiritual directors are. They are not alone in their inquiry about the nature of this ministry.

## DEFINING SPIRITUAL DIRECTION WITHIN TODAY'S CONTEXT

Contemporary writers whose work adds to the existing body of classical literature about spiritual direction offer helpful definitions for what can otherwise be difficult terminology for many to understand today. Janet Ruffing, associate professor in spirituality and spiritual direction at Fordham University, admits this difficulty.

> The classical terminology for spiritual direction is not altogether satisfactory. . . . Some people prefer to use a friendship model for spiritual direction. . . . Despite its appeal, the language of spiritual friendship neither differentiates the roles in spiritual direction nor accounts for the asymmetry that usually exists. . . . Likewise, many find the authoritarian overtones of director/directee language repugnant. Nevertheless, many people do continue to use director/directee terminology because it distinguishes the respective roles in the relationship.[5]

Along with Ruffing's call for a clarification of the respective roles within spiritual direction, a basic attitude of hospitality or receptivity belongs in the picture if we want a fuller appreciation and understanding of this time-honored ministry within the Hebrew-Christian tradition.

Not just anyone can attend to a fellow Christian's spiritual growth. Martin Thornton, an Anglican priest, points out the need for both knowledge and the experience of ascetic theology. While this theological terminology may conjure up images of large dusty volumes of books, cowled priests, and Latin chants for some of us, Thornton seeks to draw attention to the centrality of prayer.

> One calls in a plumber because he understands plumbing, not because of his wide experience of life, and one is coached by a golf professional because he is not a weekend amateur. One is suspicious

of a doctor who has read no medical book for twenty years and knows nothing of modern drugs, and I suspect that intelligent modern Christians are getting suspicious of clergy who are for ever engaged in something other than prayer. . . . It is *because* a priest has time for prayer, study and reflection that his guidance of those in the world's hurly burly is likely to be worth having.[6]

Rather than separating the ministering person from the needs of everyday life, the practice of prayer and spiritual disciplines assists her to attend to the deeper personal needs of individuals as well as the gathered congregation. Prayer and spiritual formation have a living link with everyday life and community.

Spiritual directors Sister Katherine Marie Dyckman, a Holy Names Sister, and L. Patrick Carroll, a Jesuit priest, also observe that when we speak of spiritual growth,

we do not speak of the spiritual part of the person as if that implies what is disengaged from mind and body, what is "other-worldly." Our concern is not solely, though it may at times be primarily, with what goes on in the privacy of our prayer, but with the whole of life as it leads from or leads to that prayer. All of our life . . . can be a theophany.[7]

The one who pays attention to another's spiritual growth is a seeker along with the one seeking direction for prayer—and for life as it leads from or to that prayer.[8] The director looks for and listens for the presence and guidance of the Spirit of God within the person sharing his or her story. At this point the term *director* reveals its true meaning: one who points or directs a person's attention to the presence and guidance of the Spirit of God. Sometimes when I assist someone to notice God in this way, I sense that I serve as a signpost similar to those we depend on when we travel. Signposts contain few words but do orient us to where we are and point in the right direction. Thomas Merton makes clear in his writings about spiritual direction that the Spirit of God serves as the director. (I invite you to read inclusive pronouns into the following text.)

The whole purpose of spiritual direction is to penetrate beneath the surface of a man's life, to get behind the facade of conventional gestures and attitudes which he presents to the world, and to bring out his inner spiritual freedom, his inmost truth, which is what we call the likeness of Christ in his soul. This is entirely a supernatural thing, for the work of rescuing the inner man from automatism belongs first of all to the Holy Spirit. The spiritual director cannot do such a work himself. His function is to verify and to encourage what is truly spiritual in the soul. He must teach others to "discern" between good and evil tendencies, to distinguish the inspirations of the spirit of evil from those of the Holy Spirit. A spiritual director is, then, one who helps another to recognize and to follow the inspirations of grace in his life, in order to arrive at the end to which God is leading him.[9]

Jesus speaks of the indwelling presence and work of the Holy Spirit, telling his disciples that "the Helper, the Holy Spirit, whom the Father will send in my name, will teach you everything, and remind you of all that I have said to you. . . . [H]e will guide you into all the truth" (John 14:26 [the footnote identifies "Helper" as the alternative reading for "Advocate"]; 16:13). When Simon Peter begins to realize that Jesus is the Messiah, the Son of the living God, Jesus directs Peter's attention to the source of his realization: "Blessed are you, Simon son of Jonah! For flesh and blood has not revealed this to you, but my Father in heaven" (Matt. 16:17). Jesus invites Peter to reflect on God's presence and work within him, to step back from what he has just said about who Jesus is, and to recognize God's activity and the voice of God's "honkings" within his understanding and knowing.

Throughout the scriptures we discover that God is the One who comes, who speaks, who stays in conversation with people whether they recognize it or not. The Bible contains a multitude of narratives of these conversations: God speaking and people responding. William Barry and William Connolly define spiritual direction as

help given by one Christian to another which enables that person to pay attention to God's personal communication to him or her, to respond to this personally communicating God, to grow in intimacy with this God, and to live out the consequences of the relationship.[10]

As I reflect on the felt need of persons like Jack, Mim, Hilda, or Dan who request spiritual direction for their life journey, I realize that these persons do not recognize the voice of the Spirit of God speaking to them, calling them, inviting conversation and relationship. They do not discern the "honkings" of God. But in the spiritual direction conversation, the director can help individuals to discover meaning for their awareness and experience that God is present, speaking, and calling them to "live out the consequences" of this growing relationship.

What are the consequences of spiritual direction, and how does one live them out? The ministry of spiritual direction does not happen in a vacuum. The undergirding ministries of the church also assist persons in their understanding and experience of what the call of God in Jesus is about. Tilden Edwards, an Episcopal priest, mentions several forms of authentic guidance provided by the church, including the rite of reconciliation, baptism, godparents, corporate worship, guided retreats and quiet days, the arts, reading and studying scripture, other spiritual reading, laying on of hands and anointing with oil, the ministry of small groups, seasons of the church year, prophetic preaching, relationships with other members of the church, and pastoral counseling and sustaining.[11] Sara Wenger Shenk, former pastor and now associate dean of Eastern Mennonite Seminary, includes assembling together for worship, believers' baptism, "indwelling the scriptures," the Lord's Supper, foot washing, communal discernment, conversations about faith, nonviolent love of the enemy, forgiveness and reconciliation at home, eating and singing together, church discipline, writing and telling our own stories, recovering Sunday as a day of rest, and reflecting on our practices, as she names forms and ways of guidance and nurture within the believing community.[12]

In his helpful paradigm presented below, Damien Isabell makes it clear that all ministries, activities, and relationships within the church serve to provide spiritual guidance and so direct our attention to God.[13]

SPIRITUAL DIRECTION WITHIN THE CHURCH

© 1975 by Franciscan Herald Press

When referring to *general direction of the church,* Isabell speaks of the fundamental work of spiritual direction which the church is about. He sees the church as a spiritual director since all its ministries are designed to direct the attention of its members toward the Lord. *Institutional* or *group direction* refers to all groups within the church that enable persons to grow in their relationship with God—and hence in faithfulness to God. Within our congregations we could include Sunday school classes and youth groups, Bible studies, retreats, small groups, Marriage Encounter, Cursillo and Walk to Emmaus, support groups, and the like. *One-to-one direction* refers to the work of spiritual companioning. Isabell suggests we need this kind of ministry more when the general direction of the church is weak, our theology is ambiguous, and we are making compromises with worldly values. While I agree with Isabell on this point, I am also aware that each of us seeks individual clarity about our inward journey and the outward direction of God's call in all of life. *Hidden direction* refers to the formative influence of persons on our lives, both posi-

that the Holy Spirit directs and forms us through the influence of others and the ministries of the church.

## REFLECTION

Using Isabell's diagram and explanation, reflect on the circles and the ministries of the church. In what circles have the various ministries of the church helped to direct your attention to God? How have they enabled you to grow in your love and faithfulness to God?

---

Dyckman and Carroll also pay attention to the living out of our relationship with God in their definition of spiritual direction. They specifically name the gospel as the basis for discerning how a person shapes this lived expression of intimacy with God. They describe spiritual direction as "an interpersonal relationship in which one person assists others to reflect on their own experience in the light of who they are called to become in fidelity to the Gospel."[14]

I am aware that many persons today are not familiar with the scriptures or the gospel. Significant and far-reaching reasons underlie this ignorance. If we desire to offer hospitality to persons like Hilda, Jack, Bob, Mim, Dan, and others who come seeking help in recognizing the "honkings" of God and God's presence with them, then we need listen to their stories to discover what shapes and informs their life maps and the meanings they give to their journeys. Such listening reveals the God-given-but-hidden desire for home, and uncovers whatever prevents them from engaging with the gospel.

# Attending to Spiritual Guidance

PREPARATION: Participants bring a copy of the book, a journal to write in, and their Bible to each session.

ROOM ARRANGEMENT: The person who convenes and facilitates the gathering needs to carefully choose the place and space where the group will meet. Select a space that offers privacy and freedom from ringing phones or other interruptions. Think about how to arrange the chairs and where to place a small table for a worship center. On the table place a plant, a candle, or an object that symbolizes the theme of the chapter being studied. The room arrangement assists in evoking the intent of the meeting.

TEACHING HELPS: Damien Isabell's diagram on page 25 may be copied onto a transparency and used with an overhead projector. Or reproduce Isabell's diagram on a chalkboard, whiteboard, or newsprint. Use any one of these to record the group definition of *spiritual guidance* as well.

FLOW OF THE GROUP MEETING: A guide at the end of each chapter will assist the convener and the group in planning for "Attending to Spiritual Guidance." You may use less or more than the suggested time frames, depending on the group needs.

GATHERING AND SETTLING IN (20 MINUTES)

Once people have arrived and seated themselves, start by getting to know one another. After giving names and brief biographical information, invite each person to share responses to the following questions:

- Why did you choose to be part of this learning and formation group?
- What do you desire from this group experience?
- What guidelines would help us build a sense of trust and mutuality as a group?

The responses to these three questions can become the basis for a group covenant.

MEDITATION (20 MINUTES)

Read Luke 15:11-24. Take some time to reflect on homecomings in your lives. The leader may offer these prompts for reflection:

- **Recall a memorable return home; a turning—a coming home—to God.**
- **In what way were you aware of the "honkings" of God? Who helped you hear them?**

Invite each person to share what he or she chooses from this reflection. Close in prayer.

GROUP REFLECTION (1 HOUR 10 MINUTES)

Using Damien Isabell's diagram and the explanation in this chapter, work together to name and record the various ministries, activities, and relationships within the church that can serve to provide spiritual guidance. Invite each person to share which of the church's various ministries has

- helped in directing his/her attention and life to God;
- provided spiritual guidance for his/her Christian life and walk and listening for the "honkings" of God. (35 minutes)

Direct the group to work together in pairs for the next five to ten minutes. Each pair develops a working definition of *spiritual direction/guidance* to share with the rest of the group. Then collaborate as a group to write a definition of *spiritual direction*. This statement is not final or complete but helps the group begin to express its understanding of spiritual guidance. The statement is open to revision. (35 minutes)

CLOSURE (10 MINUTES)

Gather the statements of what each person desires and needs as you meet to learn, to listen, and to pray together. Invite a volunteer to bring the statements together in the form of a covenant for the group. At a later meeting group members may review this covenant, revise as necessary, and sign it.

Remind participants as follows or in a similar vein: **In preparation for the next meeting, read chapter 2, "Recognizing the Way Our Map**

Is Drawn." Take time to respond prayerfully to the Reflection sections in this chapter and journal your responses. Again, bring your Bible, your copy of the book, and your journal to our next meeting.

Close the group session in prayer together.

Chapter 2

# Recognizing the Way Our Map Is Drawn

*Blessed are the meek, for they will inherit the earth.*
*—Matthew 5:5*

As I write I am aware of being a child of the twentieth century. I was born in England two years before the outbreak of World War II, in 1940. I was baptized into the Church of England as an infant by parents who did not otherwise attend church—along with many Britishers of that time—secure in their belief that they were Christian and thus all was well as far as religious matters were concerned. Beneath the surface of this religious nominalism and general avoidance of prayer, scripture, and other ministries of the church, another level of response to God existed.

My mother remembered her childhood experiences in vivid detail and from time to time recounted stories of her growing years to us children as we were growing up. Within this rich aural collection, several narratives revealed this deeper level of God-awareness and response. One memory centered on Sophia Anne (her mother and our grandmother), who took her and her three brothers for picnics on the South Downs, a low, undulating stretch of hills that drop off as chalk cliffs onto the stony shores of the English Channel. As mother and children sat on the scrubby grass overlooking the sea and ate toffee apples (always part of the menu), Sophia Anne would begin reciting Psalm 121 from memory. Her husband, our Grandpa Frederick, was away from home for long stretches of time, traveling in international waters as a merchant sailor. There on the hills Sophia Anne clung to the traveler's psalm, entering into the experience and faith tradition of the Hebrews who prayed and placed their trust in Yahweh during journeys full of anxiety and need. Thus my mother also learned the psalm, and would, as part of her own storytelling, begin reciting this prayer.

Her faith in God was a hidden and private affair, rarely mentioned. But then, who spoke of religious experience in those days? As a proper Britisher would have said, "It just isn't done!" And that was supposed to take care of the matter. In truth, something else informed this disconnection with the church and avoidance of talking about one's religious experience. Social practice and stigmas grow out of widely held beliefs or disbeliefs. This migration from the church and loss of language for describing personal religious experience were not sudden phenomena. Their roots were embedded in history.

## THE THEOLOGICAL AND SPIRITUAL DIVIDE

E. Rozanne Elder notes that after the twelfth century, scholasticism, a new mode of seeking to understand faith, entered the field of advanced education. Rationality began to dominate, standing over against affect; reason stood over against love; and doing over against being. A division emerged between the rational, empirical approach and the spiritual, intuitive way of knowing and responding to God.[1] At the same time, learning became scientifically organized, and academia became professional.

> The *theologian* became a specialist in an autonomous field of knowledge, which he could enter by use of a technique independent of the witness of his own life—of its personal holiness or sinfulness. The *spiritual* man, on the other hand, became a "dévot" who cared

nothing for theology, whose experience became an end in itself, without reference to any dogmatic content to be sought in it.[2]

Whereas monasteries had been the centers for learning theology, now the locus of theological study shifted to the universities as the scholastic and rationalistic method of learning about faith began to dominate acquisition of such knowledge. Early in the thirteenth century, monks started sending members of their orders to the universities to be schooled in this prevailing mode of doing theology. Without theology, devotion was to go its own way, and without devotion, theology was to dry up. During the Middle Ages, Thomas à Kempis and his Brethren of the Common Life renounced scholastic ideology.

Thus the rift deepened and widened. While the Catholic Church looked for ways to bridge the gap by insisting that ascetical, mystical, and moral theologies be included in seminary curricula, and Anglicans in the seventeenth century affirmed the basic unity between cognitive and affective ways of knowing, the rift remained. Within Protestantism there was no use for contemplative or meditative prayer, since such practice of spiritual disciplines belonged to the realm of mysticism and hence was rejected. Protestants suspected that such spiritual disciplines could be interpreted as a way of earning salvation, which smacked of merit rather than grace.

Kenneth Leech observes that this "gulf between 'academic' theology and the exercise of pastoral care and spiritual guidance has been disastrous for all concerned."[3]

> The study of theology, or at least of Christian theology, cannot survive in a healthy state apart from the life of prayer and the search for holiness. The theologian is essentially a man of prayer. . . . Theology is an encounter with the living God, not an uncommitted academic exercise. This encounter cannot survive if its only locus is the lecture theatre or the library. It needs the nourishment of sacramental worship, of solitude, of pastoral care and the cure of souls.[4]

The disaster took the shape of a reduced view of reality, growing out of the polarization between academic learning and the spiritual life. Lacking was the integration of intellect, affect, intuition, and volition. Instead, as specialists increased the segregation by focusing solely on their own specialty, reality became "frozen into one rigid 'correct view' of each of these, mistaking opinions . . . for final truth."[5] Theologians focused on academic knowledge, with no sense of connection to knowledge gained from experience of the holy; gradually theological language became severed from its roots in the theologian's personal and "experimental knowledge of God."[6] The need for an informed and discerning attention to the experience of God was forgotten and even regarded as suspect.

As a result, what we learn and know about God within our experience we are rarely able to acknowledge, and the church has little or no language to describe this experience. This lack of awareness of and language to describe spiritual experience leads to our failure to make direct connection with the lively presence of God within and behind scripture.[7] Scripture can then become just words, or as Jack described it, flat words on a flat page.

Ben Campbell Johnson notices that seminary students who expected to learn how to speak with persons about God discovered that they did not receive any guidance in that aspect of ministry.[8] Eugene Peterson, pastor, writer, and spiritual director, observes that most people assume pastors are

> teaching people to pray, helping parishioners discern the presence of grace in events and feelings, affirming the presence of God at the very heart of life, sharing a search for light through a dark passage in the pilgrimage, guiding the formation of a self-understanding that is basically spiritual instead of merely psychological or sociological.[9]

However, Peterson also exposes the gap between spiritual experience and the intellectualizing of theology when he admits that persons usually are disappointed in these assumptions about what pastors are supposed to do. As a result, we are not accustomed to speaking about spiritual formation. We have forgotten the language for speaking of our experience, and we are not even sure that experiencing God's presence and guidance is even normal. This was Dan's reason for telling me that if he described his experience of prayer, I would probably think it "weird or something." Such is the rift that has gradually but pervasively moved into our thinking, causing us to construct and live within a distorted form of reality that shuns or negates as "crazy" the presence and experience of God.

How have you learned to pray? Who taught you? How have you learned to listen to and discern your own prayer and religious experience? Recall any spiritual or prayer experiences that you have hesitated to speak of.

## THE INFLUENCE OF SECULAR BELIEF SYSTEMS

Alongside the religious divide arose secularization.

> Secularization has been a powerful movement. Those enamored by it had difficulty with the supernatural, which they have imagined as absent or remote, and to be dismantled. Secularization has emptied many churches. People have believed our world could be explained without the hypothesis of God. Dogmas were reduced to myths, and myths became fiction.[10]

This secular movement gave rise to the kind of philosophy Hilda had embraced, causing her to reject her ideas about having faith in God.

Scientific, rational, and logical modes of thinking pounded like ocean storms against what had been accepted as the safe shores of Christian orthodoxy. Empirical philosophy and language judged all that could not be measured or known through the use of the five physical senses as nonsense. While this *non-sense* is a technical term in the field of empirical philosophy, it has also became a term that minimizes the value of the emotional and spiritual, especially the latter. Gradually a skepticism dogged the language of spirituality, riddling holes in belief in the scripture and prayer as well as the need for church, congregational worship, community, and creed. While religion did not disappear, Christian orthodoxy suffered. Into its place moved psychology and other philosophical and social developments to fill the spiritual vacuum.[11]

## PSYCHOLOGY

Psychology is that insightful work with the psyche, the inner self, that aids in freeing persons from bondage to various compulsions. Here the art of listening found its lodging as persons discovered a setting where they could face their personal needs and whatever blocked fuller, freer living. In time the church began rediscovering its role of pastoral care, assisted by the empathic listening skills of psychologists, and became less critical of persons in the church who struggled in the grip of compulsive behavior. Addiction can fasten "on a work schedule, a regimen of neatness, a bedtime ritual, a diet program, on drink, drugs, or sexual obsession" and with it bring humiliation and degradation that accompanies these slavish states of being, thus living under what the apostle Paul calls principalities and powers, under totalitarian regimes.[12] Ann Ulanov maintains that even though this work with the psyche is needful, it is not completely sufficient. She sees a need to move beyond "dropping of the chains of the psyche to the taking up of the joys of the freedom of the spirit."[13] However, not all psychologists recognize the world of the spirit. Ulanov notes that instead, some within this field collapse the spiritual realm beyond and the realm within, explaining away religion by translating it into purely psychological terms.[14] Speaking from her own experience as a therapist, Ulanov points to what she calls the dangers of this young discipline:

> Depth psychology is barely a century old. It is not only young, it is often primitive in its attitudes and procedures. . . . When people get involved in it, they are gripped, fascinated, tempted to take parts for wholes. It offers one of the most alluring of the utopian diversions: everyone should be analyzed; then the world would become safe. All that is needed to explode that theory is to become an analyst, and survive in the field for twenty years or more.[15]

Thus psychologists, like other specialists, may tend to make gods rather than servants out of their science and its theories.[16]

## PLURALISM

Another way of thinking moved into the religious vacuum: pluralism. This philosophy invites a more hospitable way of seeing and responding to persons, social systems, and belief systems. It calls us to appreciate diversity and to celebrate differences. Cultural walls crumble when we understand what was once judged foreign or strange as simply different and often enriching. On the other hand, pluralism holds that nothing can be known as absolutely true.

> It is assumed that there is no place outside of culture or history from which one can derive norms of right and wrong for making a judgment. There is no absolute or universal truth but only relative and subjective truth. All belief systems are equally plausible, and all claims to truth are equally valid. No story is the only story. Truth is that which is true for *me*. Christian faith is true because some consider it true, not because it *is* true. Truth is what one feels good about. . . . Normative claims of truth are divisive, even imperialistic. Those who dogmatically appeal to revelatory authority, special insight to truth, or absolute commitments are severely criticized. They consider it a kind of idolatry to believe that truth and salvation are given decisively in Christ.[17]

Calvin Shenk, with insight informed by years of lived experience within other cultures, asks on what basis one discerns truth. He points to scripture as the starting point. Here biblical truth is not a conclusion reached as a result of human searching but rather the result of God's search for humankind. While the thirst for truth is an integral part of our human experience, Jesus points to himself as the only one who can satisfy that thirst and again to himself as "the way, the truth, and the life" (John 4:13, 14; 14:6).

Thus the biblical perspective that holds to the finality of truth in Jesus becomes a critique of relative truth. "The gospel is not one opinion among many; it is true."[18] The scriptures point to the spiritual blindness and deafness that characterize our human condition and prevent us from knowing the truth of biblical revelation (Matt. 15:12-14; Luke 4:18; John 9:35-41). As Shenk goes on to explain, people cannot be convinced by argument or assertion of biblical revelation's truth; they must recognize it. That recognition—or revelation—is enabled by the Holy Spirit.[19] Shenk calls us to immerse ourselves in scripture "so that we think in a biblically comprehensive way. . . . It is a record of God's revelation and involvement in the world, which includes God's encounter with and critique of other religions."[20]

In the book of Jeremiah we discover the discerning critique that Yahweh brings through this prophet to the people of Israel and, in turn, to us.

> Has a nation changed its gods,
>   even though they are no gods?
> But my people have changed their glory
>   for something that does not profit.
> Be appalled, O heavens, at this,
>   be shocked, be utterly desolate,
>       says the LORD,
> for my people have committed two evils:
>   they have forsaken me,
> the fountain of living water,
>   and dug out cisterns for themselves,
> cracked cisterns
>   that can hold no water (Jer. 2:11-13).

## THE INFLUENCES OF PRODUCER AND CONSUMER MATERIALISM

Forsaking God, the "fountain of living water," is demonstrated not only in our turning to other gods. Our human story, with all its goodness and beauty, is also riddled with fear, war, losses, greed, and compulsion to succeed. The secular belief systems replace our God-given identity with another. Tilden Edwards notes

> what sociologists call the rapid shift from . . . sensing a *givenness* to who we are through family, religion, and community membership, to defining ourselves (and being defined by others) in terms of what we *produce* through whatever individual way of life this production of self and things may involve. Today we also include what we *consume* as part of our identity: our consumption of education, material goods, public events, mass media, etc. Such consumptive activity can involve as much drivenness as our productivity.[21]

This individualized and driven way of life, Edwards explains, causes our need to escape. On the one hand our need to achieve, produce, and consume places enormous pressure on us. When the stress becomes too much, we tend to "collapse into some form of oblivion: sleep, drink, drugs, television, or whatever else might numb our self-production for a while."[22] Bob discovered that he had been caught up in this kind of thinking. If he did not produce what was expected of him as a pastor, then he could no longer see himself as a pastor and doubted his identity as a person. The stress of producing was wearing him down, and he sensed he was moving toward burnout as the feelings of fatigue and numbness spread within him.

This form of secular materialism grows from a deeply false belief at the core: We produce who we are; we judge ourselves worthy by what we produce and what we consume.

## REFLECTION

Take time to reflect on the influences of the secular belief systems, religious and political pluralism, and producer/consumer materialism on your life. In what ways are these belief systems contributing to the way your own life map is drawn? How are they controlling the direction your life?

## RECOGNIZING THE WAY THE MAP IS DRAWN

When persons like Hilda, Jack, Bob, Mim, and Dan call me and say that they sense a need for spiritual direction, they are reflecting the historical underpinnings of our twentieth-century context. These underpinnings inform much of the road map they are following for their life journey. The trouble is, the map lacks authentic spiritual direction, and as a result these travelers are not arriving home. Janet Ruffing points to this "historical dimension" embedded and hidden within our view of reality: "To become conscious of this reality in one's own consciousness is to acquire a historical horizon, the ability to situate one's present in relationship to the tradition or the history out of which one's own present emerges."[23]

The road map itself reveals symptoms of the deeper and more pervasive captivity, blindness, and oppression to which Jesus points and from which Jesus offers release and recovery. As he begins his work in the world, Jesus describes why he came:

> The Spirit of the Lord is upon me,
>     because he has anointed me
>         to bring good news to the poor.
> He has sent me to proclaim release to the captives
>     and recovery of sight to the blind,
>         to let the oppressed go free,
> to proclaim the year of the Lord's favor
> (Luke 4:18-19; see 4:14-21).

We are called to discover that all our stories are held and find meaning within the Great Story of God. In the next chapter we turn to this Great Story of God.

# Attending to Spiritual Guidance

## GATHERING AND SETTLING IN (15 MINUTES)

*Leader:* At the last meeting we began working on a covenant. Our covenant emerges out of our reasons for being part of this learning and formation group and our desires and needs for these sessions. We'll review our covenant toward the end of this time together.

The first reflection in chapter 1 invited us to reflect on times of homecoming in our lives: a memorable returning home and the turning and coming home to God. We recalled ways in which we have heard the "honkings" of God and remembered those who helped us hear them.

Using Damien Isabell's diagram we also spent time in group reflecting on the various ministries, activities, and relationships within the church that provide spiritual guidance. We shared which of those ministries have directed our attention to God. Part of our group meeting was also spent developing a working definition of *spiritual direction.* Here is the statement we developed.

Display the working definition of spiritual direction/guidance on a chalkboard or newsprint, read it to your group, and invite comments.

We will begin this time together by praying the scriptures. *Lectio divina*—a way of meditating on scripture—is an ancient spiritual discipline, formalized by the Benedictines in the sixth century but practiced from Old Testament times throughout the history of the church. I invite you to pray with me, asking for the guidance and help of the Spirit of God as we enter this time of sacred reading and prayerful meditation together.

*Prayer:* Holy Spirit, you are our Guide, our Helper, our Teacher. Open the ears of our souls to listen as we hear the words of Jesus. Amen.

MEDITATION (30 MINUTES)

*Lectio divina:* The leader introduces this exercise. **You will be hearing the scripture read four times. After each reading, you will receive guidance for prayerful reflection.**

> Read Matthew 11:28-30.
> *For reflection:* **Hear Jesus' invitation to come.** (Pause.)
> Read Matthew 11:28-30.
> *For reflection:* **As you come to Jesus, pay attention to how the yoke of the world—all its belief systems and demands—weighs upon you and tires you.** (Pause.)
> Read Matthew 11:28-30.
> *For reflection:* **Listen to Jesus' invitation to you to lay down what burdens you and tires you. Notice what you lay down and how Jesus responds to you.** (Pause.)
> Read Matthew 11:28-30.
> *For reflection:* **Jesus offers you a comfortable yoke, a way of *being* that is light and easy, giving you rest.**

> **Be in the presence of Jesus now, and be aware of how you respond to his invitation.** (Pause.) **Working in pairs, take five minutes each listening to the other's experience of practicing *lectio divina.***

GROUP REFLECTION (1 HOUR)

The leader poses the following questions for the group.

- How are you aware of the history embedded in your own story?
- What is life-giving in your history?
- How are the ideologies of empirical learning, psychology, religious and political pluralism, and producer/consumer materialism shaping your thinking and directing how you live?
- What do these approaches offer that is helpful, life-giving?
- In what ways do they give false direction?
- How has the history of division between our ways of knowing affected how we recognize and discern God's presence and work?
- How do we listen as we are engaged in pastoral care, teaching,

preaching, leading worship, praying, listening to our own spiritual experience?

Allow time for group conversation.

## CLOSURE (15 MINUTES)

Pass out copies of the group covenant for persons to read and respond to. Take time to hear any suggestions for changes that need to be considered.

For our next group gathering, read chapter 3, "Paying Attention to Story and the Great Story." Again take time to respond prayerfully to the Reflection sections and journal your responses. Bring your Bible, your copy of the book, and your journal to our next meeting.

Close in prayer.

# Chapter 3

# Paying Attention to Story and the Great Story

*The LORD has been mindful of us; he will bless us; . . .*
*both small and great.—Psalm 115:12-13*

As people we are storytellers, and we enjoy listening to the stories of others. We live our lives immersed in stories as we watch the news, read the paper, listen to family members tell about their day, read a book, or watch a movie. A good story draws us into the reality and experience of the persons within it. Stories also creep into our soul, speaking to forgotten and lost pieces of our experience, waking them from slumber and inviting them to walk into the light of our conscious awareness. At ten years of age, I wept inconsolably while watching the film *Pinocchio*, and my parents finally took me out of the movie house. Only years later did I realize why this story of a runaway puppet who wanted to become real evoked such a grief-filled response within me. This story had given me meaning and permission for the grief and tears I had not been able to express when I was separated from my parents and siblings at five years of age during the World War II bombing raids on London. However, the story also spoke on a deeper, spiritual level. I felt drawn toward God but knew intuitively that I had no power over whatever pulled me away from my ultimate home in God's presence. The tears welled up from a place of deep lostness and longing.

## THE GREAT STORY

The Hebrew-Christian tradition comes to us through story. The Bible is a book of stories. Here we find the story of our beginning, of God and creation, and here we discover the story of losing our way after being lured into believing a glittering web of lies spun by the great archenemy of our souls (Genesis 3). Here we find meaning for our sense of lostness and existential loneliness. And here we are drawn into the stories of God's coming, the continual "honkings" of God, calling our name, inviting us to return home—to God, to ourselves, and to one another.[1] The scriptures also offer stories of our response to God's coming—accounts of resistance and avoidance, for we war with God, others, and ourselves even while we long for peace. Buried beneath our hostilities is a desire for peace with God, for friendship in this world, and for home—that secure shelter where we and all persons can be received, named, nurtured, and adequately fed. In the biblical narrative we discover the Great Story within which our lives and our stories are held. We have a universal need for such a story that tells us who we are and where we are, who God is, and how we relate to the world and all that is.[2]

The biblical storytellers pay attention to God behind and within all the narratives. "Behind the fight for existence, the trance within, and the heavens above, the narrator places God. The Other is present in shelter, food, clothes, dread, and struggle."[3] In a sense, all stories, no matter who tells them and when they are told, tell the same story—of our flight from God and our return to God.[4] The Bible tells the story of God coming to us in many different ways but always with the same invitation to return to the fountain and source of our life and being. The Gospels contain the Great Story of God coming to us in Jesus, inviting us home. God shows up here, among us.

## THE PASTORAL TASK OF SPIRITUAL COMPANIONING

Now most of us have trouble with God's showing up, especially at our own front door. We may be like Mim who said that God was "such an ogre" for her, One who would not accept her if she ventured closer. If this is our attitude, we tend to keep our front door shut tight against any heavenly visitations. Or, like Bob, we keep busy, very busy, always on the run and thus never at home if God comes to call. Or, like Dan, we may have the furniture within our living room arranged according to the rules of our social and religious tradition and be quite settled in knowing how God comes and what God expects. But when God shows up in the attic, the basement, or other unexpected places, our rules don't seem to work any more. The tradition that shapes us and draws our life maps is too small to contain or explain the new experience of God. Like Dan, we may even wonder if we are "weird or something." If the scriptures have been flat words on a flat page, as with Jack, we may even resist any thought of paying attention to the Gospels. Like Zechariah, in Luke's account, we may need a heavenly visitor to help us see beyond and through our resistance and unbelief (Luke 1).

The gospel narrators are familiar with this sense of longing as well as feelings of dis-ease and varied responses to the divine. Like us, they live this side of Eden. They know from their own experience as well as from others' stories how slowly people catch on to what this divine visitation is about. Within the gospel story they reveal their own pre-understandings of who Jesus is and why he came. Simon Peter remembers his response to Jesus after hauling in a miraculous catch of fish; he tells Jesus, "Go away from me, Lord, for I am a sinful man!" He is quite sure that Jesus sees him as sinful and fears Jesus' coming too close (Luke 5:8).

All who have been following Jesus expect him to reclaim the monarchy, to be installed on the throne of David, and to restore the political fortunes of Israel—and their personal fortunes along with him. This pre-understanding of the early disciples arises out of their national and religious story. Hence, when Jesus begins to speak of suffering, death, and resurrection they are unable to receive what he is saying (Matt. 16:21-22;

Mark 9:30-32; Luke 9:44-45). Only later, when they look back with the help of an understanding and revelation given them by Jesus and enlightenment from the Holy Spirit, can they perceive and understand the meaning of God's coming in Jesus.[5] However, the gospel narrators choose to tell the story as they experienced it at the time—as men and women caught in the web of distorted messianic expectations. As we listen to their telling of the story of Jesus, of God's coming, we also hear accounts of other persons who gathered around Jesus: narratives of rejection, disbelief, limited understanding, questioning, wonder, doubt, healing, and faith. Our gospel hosts invite us to become aware of how much we—like they and others they encounter—also struggle to believe.

First they lay out the story as historians, "searching out the story from beginning to end and creating an interpretive narrative that shows the coherence and meaning of the story." Our gospel hosts, however, also pay attention to the pastoral work of showing concern for the individual and how each person (including themselves) finds purpose and meaning in the context of the Great Story.[6] To do this ministry of spiritual companioning, the gospel writers listen deeply to the Holy Spirit and to their own and others' responses to God's showing up in Jesus.[7]

These pastoral storytellers show Jesus serving as the spiritual director. They continually point toward Jesus and his way of receiving and responding to people along with how the map of their external and inner experience is drawn and lived. The gospel narrators become our spiritual companions, inviting us into the Great Story in order to receive spiritual guidance from Jesus for our own journey.

## ASSISTANCE IN ENTERING THE BIBLICAL STORY

These narrators help us to enter the gospel story. Their guidance serves to secure the path as we walk past the rationally bound gods of reason, science, and intellectual pursuit that, though serving us well, have defined rather narrowly the role and importance of learning from personal experience and the Spirit of God. These followers of Jesus also offer us new ways of seeing as they collaborate with Jesus to bring healing from secular and worldbound views that blindfold our ability to discern the existence of God and the spiritual dimension of our own story (Luke 4:16-21). As we accept this invitation from the gospel narrators to enter into the Great Story, we will discover a place where these false divisions gradually are mended and where all our ways of learning and knowing become servants of God. In this way we learn to love God with all of our heart, soul, mind, and strength.

What kind of help do the narrators give, and how do we recognize their messages? Some of their help is hidden and, like forgotten and submerged parts of our storied experience, lies buried within the text of the story. Unless we are students of Greek and various literary devices, we will not notice the invitations from our gospel companions. However, the work of biblical scholars brings these small but important invitations to light.

## USE OF THE HISTORICAL PRESENT

The gospel writers make fairly frequent use of the historical present, a verb tense used in the Greek but not in English. For example, in Mark 10:46 and 10:49, most English versions translate the Greek verb (which is in the historical present) into the past tense: "They came to Jericho."

However, our gospel companion and narrator desires to invite our presence at the event. Thus Mark uses the historical present tense, which should be translated: "They come to Jericho."

This small literary device snags our attention and draws us into the scene, places us on the road along with Jesus, the disciples, the crowd, and a blind beggar named Bartimaeus. Then, when Jesus stops to listen to this blind man's plea for mercy and help, we are also addressed: Jesus stood still and said, "Call him here." And they call [historical present] the blind man, saying to him, "Take heart; get up, he is calling you" (v. 49).

We discover that Jesus also turns to us and asks, "What do you want me to do for you?" Now the gospel event is no longer some distant happening in an ancient city, concerning people we never knew. We are face-to-face with Jesus who stands before us, inviting us to tell him what we desire him to do for us.

Our travel guides know that the gospel is the Story for all people—past, present, and future. Their use of the historical present transports the listener and reader into the actual scene by bringing us into the actual time of the event.[8]

Most readers of the Gospels are quite unaware of the use of the historical present, since committees of New Testament translators usually hold the view that translating words in this tense would result in an uneven English translation.[9] Translators of the New American Standard Bible decided to mark with an asterisk (*) each instance of the historical present in the gospel accounts. In this case, we discover how scholarship can become a servant of the gospel story, allowing us to hear the welcome our gospel narrators offer.

## USE OF VARIOUS GREEK WORDS FOR SIGHT OR SEEING

Another means of invitation is the use of various Greek words for *sight* or *seeing*. John uses five different words. One of these, *theasthai*, can be translated "contemplate," which, according to G. L. Phillips, means "to look at some dramatic spectacle and in a measure to become a part of it."[10] John Koenig, professor of New Testament at General Theological Seminary, explains that this use hints at what the gospel reader always is to do.[11] In his gospel, the disciple John records this intent when he says, "Look around you, and see how the fields are ripe for harvesting" (John 4:35). Here Jesus calls us to stand alongside him as he contemplates the need for persons to invite others into God's gracious kingdom and rule. Thus we also are called to see, to contemplate, and thus to enter into what is happening within the gospel narrative.

This act of contemplation is a receptive, humble way of seeing. Here we are invited to wait, to look in unhurriedly, and to depend on the Holy Spirit's presence within and behind the scripture to help us perceive what is being made known to us. Reading becomes prayer, and prayer becomes attentive listening and contemplation as we meet and are met by Jesus.

Due to our rational tendency to analyze and outline the text, we are not accustomed to reading the scriptures in this way. However, today we are uncovering these invitations in the scriptures and discovering their use across the centuries in the practice of the church. In the early Middle Ages, illustrated editions of the Gospels offered guidance to enter the gospel. Numerous pen-drawings accompanied the text, assisting persons who could not read. These pictorial Gospels included instructions to help the reader slow down and begin to notice who was present in the story and what was happening. The pictures and instructions brought the reader into the story to be present and participate and to be present to Jesus.[12]

## REFLECTION

*Practicing the Spiritual Discipline of Entering the Story.* Engage all your senses as you enter the story below. See the place and the people present. Feel the ground beneath your feet, the warmth of the sun on your head and shoulders. Notice what you smell, what you taste. Pay attention to what you touch—and what you avoid touching. Notice who touches you. Listen to what is said. Look, contemplate, gaze upon what you see.

Our gospel companion, Mark, invites us to be present on the beach near Capernaum. Jesus and the disciples have just returned from a trip across the lake, and as they moor the boat, a crowd gathers around them.

Read the narrative below from Mark 5:22-24, 35-43 (AP) twice, the first time without pausing. Italicized words indicate use of the historical present. During the second reading, pause for about twenty seconds at caret signs (^) in the text.

> Then one of the leaders of the synagogue named Jairus *comes* and, when he *sees* him, *falls* at his feet and *begs* him repeatedly, "My little daughter is at the point of death. Come and lay your hands on her, so that she may be made well, and live."^ So he goes with him. . . . [S]ome people *come* from the leader's house to say, "Your daughter is dead. Why trouble the teacher any further?" But overhearing what they said, Jesus *says* to the leader of the synagogue, "Do not fear, only believe." ^ He *allows* no one to follow him except Peter, James and John, the brother of James. When they *come* into the house of the leader of the synagogue, he *sees* a commotion, people weeping and wailing loudly. When he has entered, he *says* to them, "Why do you make a commotion and weep? The child is not dead but sleeping." And they *laugh* at him. ^ Then he *puts* them all outside, and *takes* the child's father and mother and those who were

51

with him, and goes in where the child was. ^ He *takes* her by the hand and *says* to her, "*Talitha cum*," which means, "Little girl, *get up!*" ^ And immediately the girl gets up and begins to walk about (she is twelve years of age). At this they are overcome with amazement. He . . . tells them to give her something to eat.

*Discernment.* Allow ten minutes for prayerful reflection as you enter the gospel narrative. Where do you find yourself in relationship to Jesus, the crowd, and the parents of the little girl?

What has fallen asleep or has died in your own life? (It could be your sense of call, your experience of joy in serving God, energy in ministry or in certain areas of your life and relationships).

How do you respond when Jesus tells you, "Do not fear, only believe"? Jesus comes closer now and takes you by the hand, inviting that which has died or is sleeping to wake up: *"Talitha cum!"* What do you notice? In what way are you being invited to nurture and feed this part of your life?

———⚬———

## USE OF DIRECT SPEECH

The use of direct speech allows us to sense that Jesus is directly addressing us along with the crowds and the disciples. The gospel writers include Jesus' use of imperatives along with his direct address, using the pronoun "you" rather than the more indirect "they" or "them." In this way we hear Jesus directing us to "ask, and it will be given you; search, and you will find; knock, and the door will be opened for you" (Matt. 7:7). We are thus "summoned to hear and internalize Jesus' speeches" and so "be conformed to the shape of his life."[13]

This close listening moves into meditation as we allow the words of Jesus to move slowly into deeper levels of our awareness and being, speaking to the hidden and submerged parts of our storied experience. Here *lectio divina,* that ancient spiritual discipline of meditation on the scriptures happens.

## REFLECTION

Practicing the spiritual discipline of *lectio divina* assists us to hear, to listen to God not just on a surface level but with the heart, that inner place of our will, thinking, feeling, memory, being, and spirit.[14]

*Preparation.* After a prayer for openness to God, turn to the text:

> "The one who enters by the gate is the shepherd of the sheep. The gatekeeper opens the gate for him, and the sheep hear his voice. He calls his own sheep by name and leads them out . . . and the sheep follow him because they know his voice." . . . Jesus said to them, . . . "I am the gate for the sheep. . . .Whoever enters by me will be saved, and will come in and go out and find pasture. . . . I am the good shepherd. I know my own and my own know me" (John 10:2-4, 7, 9, 14).

Read the text, stopping when a word or phrase stands out for you. This awareness may not be strong, but when a word or phrase catches your attention, stay there.

Meditate on the word or phrase. Repeat it to yourself several times. Reflect on its meaning. Allow the word to sink gradually to deeper levels of your awareness and to enter into all the rooms of your life and experience.

*Respond to God in prayer.* Speak to God about your discoveries as God uses the word from scripture to read your life.

*Be still.* Simply rest in the spacious and gracious presence of God.

*Discernment.* How has God's presence surprised you through praying the scripture? What word or phrase invited your attention? In what way did this word open up its meaning for you? In what way did it speak to your life?

———◉———

# COMPASSION FOR THE KNOWN AND THE HIDDEN IN OUR STORY

If we are slow and resistant to God's work in our lives as we walk this soul and life journey, we will discover that we are not alone. Our disciple companions share their own experience of receiving spiritual guidance from Jesus during bouts of little faith, fear, dislocation, desire for power, disloyalty, disbelief, anxiety, sadness, and terror as well as during movement toward trust, insight, and obedience. This dual experience of being companioned by narrators who tell their own story and by Jesus who invites us to come as we are assures us of empathy and compassion: We may allow the many and various parts of our story—known and hidden—to come into the light of Jesus' presence.

Empathic listening is a receptive hospitality, a making of space for other individuals and their storied experience. In this hospitable space people feel free to explore their experiences, to tell their stories. Empathic listening allows us as listeners to "reach the internal array of another's experience." Ruthellen Josselson also observes that this "internal array" includes the self in dialogue with itself.[15] Parts of the self may be hidden but will reveal themselves within the story the person is telling as conflicting material emerges. Susan Chase refers to this hidden and possible conflicting material as "submerged stories" and invites our attention to those fragments of story that emerge through the cracks of the larger narrative.[16] I once listened to a woman whose husband had died a few months before. Betty was eighty-two and had enjoyed a long and good relationship with her husband, Elmer. As we sat together, enjoying hot herbal tea on a cold November day, Betty began telling me how she was doing since Elmer's death. "God is good, really good. I have so much to be thankful for. Each morning I wake up and think of all the good things in my life. I have so much joy and strength." She paused, was quiet for a few moments, and then said, "Sometimes I don't sleep very well, but I praise God for those times too. God is so good. I'm going for walks when the weather permits. And I'm still quilting some." She paused again and then said, "I don't know what I would do if I didn't keep my hands busy."

"It helps you to have something to do?" I asked.

"God helps me. I have such strength, and I'm thankful to God for that."

As Betty shared her story, I realized that some painful submerged pieces of her experience slipped through here and there as she talked. It would be a while before Betty would be ready to talk about her feelings of loss, grief, and loneliness.

In the gospel narratives we will be paying attention to the "internal array" of persons like Simon Peter, listening carefully to his "submerged story" of fear and anxiety which Jesus notices and brings to light. As these submerged stories do come to light, not only does the self communicate with its various parts but the Holy Spirit is also present. God is in dialogue with Peter and with us. The pastoral work of spiritual companioning pays attention to this dialogue of God with our stories—known and hidden—and to our response to God in the light of the Great Story.

# Attending to Spiritual Guidance

### GATHERING AND SETTLING IN (15 MINUTES)

*Leader:* **At our last group meeting we reviewed our covenant.**

Pass out copies of the revised group covenant, invite persons to read it through, then to participate in signing the covenant together. Offer the covenant to God in prayer.

**At our last group meeting we also reviewed a working definition of *spiritual direction*, practiced the spiritual discipline *lectio divina*, reflected on the history within our own personal stories, and paid attention to the way in which the division between our ways of knowing affect our lives and ministry today.**

**Today we will begin our time together by praying the scriptures. This time we will be entering the gospel story, using the guidance offered in chapter 3 of our text (Mark 5:22-24, 35-43). I invite you to pray with me, asking for the guidance and help of the Spirit of God as we enter the gospel narrative.**

*Prayer:* **Loving and gracious God, thank you for bringing us together again. As your servants and followers of Jesus, help us by your Holy Spirit as we engage with the gospel narrative. Open the eyes of our souls to see, the ears of our hearts to hear, in the name of Jesus Christ. Amen.**

### MEDITATION (30 MINUTES)

*Entering the Narrative*

Use the Reflection section "Practicing the Spiritual Discipline of Entering the Story" in this chapter. Read the first part of the section, then read the passage in Mark 5:22-24, 35-43 twice. Use the guidance offered here to lead the group into the narrative. Read slowly and allow pauses where shown (^) for persons to encounter and to be encountered by the story. The discernment component allows ten minutes of silent meditation followed by questions for private consideration. After a few minutes reflection, invite the group to share their experiences of entering the gospel narrative.

## GROUP REFLECTION (1 HOUR 10 MINUTES)

Invite group members to remember and share the name of a story that has been meaningful in their own life. Now ask people to reflect on biblical stories. In what way do one or two biblical narratives draw their attention and speak to their soul? (15 minutes)

Entering the narrative of scripture can be a new experience for some people. Invite discussion about how gospel narrators invite the listener or reader to walk into the story (10–15 minutes).

Spend the next twenty minutes working in pairs telling stories and listening. One person will choose an experience from his or her life and soul journey to share and the other will be the listener. The person listening is invited to companion his/her partner with compassion and empathy while listening to the content, feelings, signs of God's presence and work, and layers of meaning within the storyteller's experience. (See Reflection below on sharing story and serving as listener to story.)

Following twenty minutes in pairs, return to group and share your experiences (20 minutes).

*Reflection for the person sharing his or her story:*
What did you notice as you shared your experience?
In what ways did you feel truly heard, empathized with?

*Reflection for the person companioning:*
What feelings did you notice within as you served as listener?
What was happening within yourself?
In what way were you open to God?
How did you respond to the person's story?

- Open, receptive listening
- Empathy with the person and his or her experience
- Avoidance of listening and being present to the other's experience and feelings

- Asking God for help, being open to God as you listened
- Starting to tell your own story
- Becoming theological
- Other

## CLOSURE (5 MINUTES)

*Leader:* Today we began our time of attending to spiritual guidance by entering into covenant together. We engaged with the scriptures by entering the gospel narrative. In our group work we paid attention to stories which have been meaningful in our lives, and we spent time listening to each others' stories. We also reflected on our experience of sharing our experience and of being listeners.

In preparation for our next time together, read chapter 4, "Beginning the Journey." Again take time to respond prayerfully to the Reflection sections in this chapter and to journal your responses. Bring your Bible, your copy of the book, and your journal to our next meeting.

Close with a benediction.

Chapter 4

# Beginning the Journey

*Go from your country and your kindred . . . to the land
I will show you. . . . and I will bless you, . . . so that
you will be a blessing.—Genesis 12:1-2*

We begin our journey now into the world of the Gospels with Mark's Gospel, our primary guidebook, in hand. As you read Mark 1:1-11, ask the Holy Spirit to help you enter the story. You start this pilgrimage on the east bank of the Jordan River, just north of the Dead Sea and near Bethany. A crowd of people is also gathered here by the shores of the Jordan: mothers holding their children, fathers, Roman soldiers, tax collectors for the Romans, and some priests and Levites from Jerusalem. They are wanting to hear John the Baptist who preaches and baptizes here at the Jordan.

This ancient river, fed by springs and streams from Mount Hermon in the north, has its own story to tell. These banks carry memories of another crowd whose feet stood on the eastern slopes, wondering how they would cross over into Canaan. The Israelite people had spent 430 years in Egypt, having become slaves to the Egyptian pharaohs before Yahweh rescued them. Then followed that long and terrifying journey through the desert, made all the longer by the people's fear of crossing over the Jordan into Canaan. Who knew what awaited them there? Other giants of power and death? And so they had turned back and wandered in the desert—always attended by Yahweh in the cloud by day and in the bright pillar of fire glowing in the darkness of those desert nights. Finally there they stood again at the Jordan, waiting to cross over.

The priests went ahead of them bearing the ark—that great and awesome dwelling place of God's presence—wading into the swift waters. As if a great unseen hand were holding the river in check, the flow of water slowed to a halt and began to draw back upon itself. The riverbed became a road for the Israelites to take into the land of promise. What a crossing that was—a homecoming after two generations of desert wandering. And what a people and nation they had become! There were no equals to their kings or their temple.

But what had begun as a broad and wonderful promise of fulfillment sank slowly into a narrow grind of existence. Now a military and political world power occupied their land. Roman soldiers stood on every corner; tax collectors demanded money at every turn, persistent reminders of Rome's domination.

Farmers who worked the fields of the hill country found themselves at risk. Often lack of rain or an infestation of insects resulted in meager harvests. Roman taxes cut deep into their slim earnings. Some survived by selling themselves into the service of wealthier landowners or even turning to robbery in order to buy food.[1] The joy and freedom of the kingdom under David was no longer known. Yes, there had been uprisings, brave men who had stood against Greek and Roman domination. But it would take someone with miraculous powers to restore the kingdom, to unseat the Roman governor who had authority over Herod—a king but a puppet to his own selfish whims and to the Roman authorities.

In the midst of daily labor framed by the demeaning and uneasy occupation by the Romans, a voice begins to sound. At first in the wilderness of Judea, then closer, on the banks of this river, as if somehow it knew the road from slavery and wandering. Now at the banks of the Jordan River, this voice offers promise and homecoming: "Repent, turn around! You'll get lost traveling in that direction. Turn back, for the kingdom of heaven is here, close by" (Mark 1:15, AP).

The people are ready for prophets like those in earlier times who had announced Yahweh's victory over the enemy. They recall Daniel's foretelling of God's power over those who oppressed Israel and the establishment of an everlasting kingdom by God for the righteous (Dan. 6:26; 7:14). They delight to hear this rough-looking man in a camel-hair tunic order tax collectors to collect no more than the amount prescribed, tell Roman soldiers to stop extorting money by threat or false accusation, and instruct soldiers not to ask for a raise in pay. And they are startled by John the Baptist's response when they ask, "What then should we do?" Standing there in the river, water dripping from his brown skin and tunic, John says, "Whoever has two coats must share with anyone who has none; and whoever has food must do likewise" (Luke 3:10-11).

All eyes of the crowd are riveted on him. People wonder if this could be the one sent from God to save them, their land, their nation. But John announces: "I baptize you with water. Among you stands one whom you do not know, the one who is coming after me; I am not worthy to untie the thong of his sandal" (Luke 3:16).

His dark eyes search among the crowd. Some have been baptized in the Jordan by John. Their hair and clothes cling to their wet skin, warmed now by the afternoon sun.

Quietly, almost unnoticed, a man begins to move from the back of the crowd. He walks down the bank and wades into the river to be baptized. John assists him into the waters of the Jordan. As the man emerges from the water, he raises his hands in prayer, and he looks up to the sky. The skies have been drawn back, as though an unseen hand has pulled aside the shimmering curtain of blue, revealing heaven! Shining, light, beautiful, inviting. The waters of the river have not parted, but heaven has been opened. A dove descends from this shining beauty, wings its way downward to the place where all stand transfixed, and gently settles on the shoulder of this man who stands in front of John. Another voice sounds, but not from the wilderness. This voice speaks from heaven: "You are my Son, the Beloved; with you I am well pleased" (Mark 1:11; Luke 3:22).

## REFLECTION

Enter into this narrative from the Gospels. Spend time on the banks of the Jordan River. Wade into the water and be present as the heavens part. Listen as God says to Jesus, "This is my beloved Son! With you I am well pleased." Listen as God says to you, "This is my beloved daughter/son! With you I am well pleased."

---

## WILDERNESS SOLITUDE

At first glance it seems that Jesus could have taken advantage of the heavenly revelation complete with God's speaking directly to him in the presence of the waiting crowd. What power and prestige he could claim! How the people would listen and believe! He has been sent by God to be the Savior of the world. This is his mission. But how will he begin this work? What approach should he take? How will he bring good news to these crowds of poor, hungry people, dominated and harassed by those with wealth and military might? How can he help them see God's love and care, when the religious leaders have turned the Mosaic law and its many traditions into a tight and constrictive system that demands their constant attention? How can he turn their attention toward heart and spirit when the daily struggle for life and survival dominate their vision? He is the Son of God! Doesn't that count for something? Isn't God about saving this world and these people? But the Spirit of God does not lead Jesus toward the people and their multiple needs. Not yet.

## Reflection

Listen prayerfully as you hear and enter the gospel in Mark 1:12-13 and Luke 4:1-13 where Luke comes alongside to add some detail.

> And the Spirit immediately drove him out into the wilderness. He was in the wilderness forty days, tempted by Satan; and he was with the wild beasts; and the angels waited on him.

After Jesus had spent forty days fasting, a voice sounds in the great silence of the wilderness: "If you are the Son of God, command this stone to become a loaf of bread." Jesus looks around at the stones scattered on the ground of the wilderness floor. Yes, they could become loaves of bread! How the hungry and poor would like to be fed! He could prove his power and identity so easily. But in quiet of wilderness solitude, he has learned to be present to the inner space of his soul. There he discerns the Spirit drawing his attention to the evil intent of the devil's offer, and he remembers his people's experience of wilderness and hunger.

> Remember the long way that the LORD your God has led you these forty years in the wilderness, in order to humble you, testing you to know what was in your heart, whether or not you would keep his commandments. He humbled you by letting you hunger, then by feeding you with manna, with which neither you nor your ancestors were acquainted, in order to make you understand that one does not live by bread alone, but by every word that comes from the mouth of the LORD (Deut. 8:2-3).

He would trust God to provide manna in the wilderness of people's lives. Human hungers are a sign of deeper hunger—hunger for God and God's ways. Bread alone can never satisfy their soul.

The devil begins to lead Jesus higher up the mountain slopes to heights beyond the peaks of the wilderness ranges. In a brilliant flash, Satan shows him all the kingdoms of the world.

> To you I will give their glory and all this authority; for it has been given over to me, and I give it to anyone I please. If you, then, will worship me, it will all be yours (Luke 4:6).

The kingdoms, each with its strata of political systems and powers, lie within his grasp. What if he were enthroned king as the triumphal messiah? What freedom he could bring to the world! All the powers of political rule which burdened and bent the backs of rich and poor, men and women, slave and free, Roman and Greek, Jew and Gentile, could be his to bring goodness and release to all! But the tail of the serpent is exposed in this glittering offer: " . . . if you worship me."

Jesus remembers the people standing east of the Jordan hundreds of years before, listening as Moses recited the Shema before they crossed over into the Promised Land. Now Jesus speaks these beloved words that have been food for his soul.

> Hear, O Israel: The LORD is our God, the Lord alone. You shall love the LORD your God with all your heart, and with all your soul, and with all your might (Deut. 6:4-5).

Quite suddenly the shimmering illusion of political glory vanishes, and again Jesus is standing on the rocky ground of the Judean wilderness. But the devil is not done. Not yet.

Jesus feels himself swept upward, transported by an ill spiritual wind which deposits him on the pinnacle of the temple in Jerusalem. The Adversary continues, "if you are the Son of God, throw yourself down from here, for it is written, 'He will command his angels concerning you, to protect you,' and 'On their hands they will bear you up, so that you will not dash your foot against a stone'" (Luke 4:9-11).

How true! But how darkly subtle! To lure Jesus into doing the spectacular in order to prove God is present. Like Moses, Jesus will wait on God in simple trust to act and reveal God's self, even while the people quarrel and test Yahweh, saying, "Is the LORD among us or not?" (Exod. 17:1-7). He knows it is the work of the devil to blind the soul to God's presence. Jesus confronts Satan now with simplicity and directness: "Do not put the Lord your God to the test." The devil leaves.

Weak and tired, Jesus waits in the silence of that deserted place. Angels come, bringing food, waiting on him. Abba is setting a table in the wilderness.

## REFLECTION

Reflect on times in your life when you have been led into the wilderness—times of silence, absence, testing; seasons when God seemed distant.

The invitation of the wilderness is to wait, to allow the various parts of our selves to wear themselves out arguing, debating, and figuring out ways of escape. In time they tire and sit down on the ground. There the grip of the powers and structures of this world's system begin to loosen as we—like Jesus—see them for what they are in this place beyond structures. We become still and quiet in the solitude of silence and absence. The interior space of our soul is gentled into a restful and hospitable readiness for Yahweh and for the Spirit's guidance to help us know how the kingdom of God comes. These are the gifts of the wilderness.

---

## EARLY ENCOUNTERS

John's disciples wonder how they will recognize the messiah when he comes. John the Baptist admits he had the same question. "I myself did not know him, but the one who sent me to baptize with water said to me, 'He on whom you see the Spirit descend and remain is the one who baptizes with the Holy Spirit.' And I myself have seen and have testified that this is the Son of God." The next day, as he stands with two followers, John becomes aware that Jesus is walking by and says, "Look, here is the Lamb of God!" (John 1:33, 35).

Two of John's disciples (John and Andrew) hear him and follow Jesus. Jesus turns, sees them following, and says, "What are you looking for?" They say to him, "Rabbi, where are you staying?" He replies, "Come and see." They go and see where he is staying, and they remain with him that day. It is about four o'clock in the afternoon. (See John 1:33-39.)

# SPIRITUAL DIRECTION: BEING RECEPTIVE TO THE HUNGERS AND DESIRES OF OTHERS

As we enter this narrative the first words Jesus speaks to us come in the form of a question: "What are you looking for?" This kind of open-ended question invites reflection rather than a simple yes or no response, which sometimes shuts down exploration. Rather than telling these disciples of John the Baptist what he knows they are about, Jesus asks them to tell him. Here begins the journey of self-disclosure—to know oneself and to be known by Jesus. In his ministry of spiritual direction, Jesus could discern what was within persons—what motivated and drove them to action, to resistance, to response. He had faced his own testing in the wilderness and knew the ways in which desires could be enticed and inflamed within the human heart. However, Jesus did not always speak what he discerned; instead, he responded in a way that assisted the person in learning the art of discernment—knowing one's own inner heart and interior. Hence his question, "What are you looking for?" Jesus could wait, even while he trusted God to be at work in the lives of these men.

At first these two disciples give what may sound like a surface response born out of curiosity and their desire to know how to find this rabbi on a later day: "Rabbi, where are you staying?" (What is your street address, e-mail address, and phone number? How can we get in touch with you again?)

Jesus responds by accepting these two seekers for who they are and within the limits of their understanding. He offers an invitation: "Come and see." Such an act of listening and responding grows out of receptive hospitality toward the other person. Listening does not imply that we lose our sense of who we are or our call to bring good news. Genuine receptivity brings grace along with good news. Grace does not limit truth telling nor deny the truth but rather creates a space into which the other person may bring his or her own self and desires. Grace also invites the other to bring his or her limited awareness into the shelter of the Greater Story of God in Jesus, the Way, the Truth, and the Life. In the context of this Story, ongoing conversion and transformation can gradually happen.

After spending some time with Jesus, these disciples of John the Baptist are able to express what they are looking for:

> One of the two who heard John speak and followed [Jesus] was Andrew, Simon Peter's brother. He first found his brother Simon and said to him, "We have found the Messiah" (John 1:40-41).

For these early followers, their expectation—or their prejudgment—of Jesus will surface sometimes in words, sometimes in action. But it is there, within and behind all their experiences of following Jesus, and it will color and distort how they understand what Jesus is about. All of us have only this limited knowledge of Jesus' mission. A deeper, unspoken expectation exists within the disciples and within us. And so this question Jesus asks—What are you looking for?—is a question that they and we learn to live with. It is a soul question, evoking our own limited truth and calling on us to discover the Greater Truth Jesus offers.

Jack, the social worker who desired to know Jesus, admitted that he expected Jesus either to take care of the church in the way he cleansed the temple (sweeping away all that is out of order, unfinished, immature, and unloving) or to eliminate the church altogether. Jack saw himself as a true caregiver for persons in great need: compassionate, healing, listening, and finding answers to impossible questions within the system. Attending church was out of the question for him. He was too angry and kept his distance. Like James and John, he would have liked to call down fire upon congregations who had not been understanding and hospitable to the needy individuals Jack saw in his office.

But Jack knew Jesus cared—at least for the clients he met with. But he experienced love in a rather tight circle—among Jesus and these individuals. Somehow, even though Jack wasn't sure about his own relationship with Jesus, Jack was involved. His understanding of love was not large enough, though, to embrace all humankind—churched and nonchurched—as needy and in need of God's love and care.

Hence Jack's statement as he first explained what he was looking for in spiritual direction: "I want to know who this Jesus is for myself. He can do something for me that I see him doing for my clients." And this is where Jesus met him, on an individual basis for a while. Gradually Jesus worked with Jack's blind spots and the narrow pathways within his under-standing, bringing healing, light, and freedom from painful and negative experiences, shedding light on false thinking. In time Jesus drew Jack's atten-tion to his need to find a community of persons who were also followers, seeking God and God's loving ways in the world of their lives and work.

# Attending to Spiritual Guidance

## GATHERING AND SETTLING IN (10 MINUTES)

*Leader:* **During our last time together we attended to story—stories meaningful in our own lives and the biblical story. We experienced the spiritual discipline of entering the gospel narrative and spent time one-on-one listening to each other's soul journey. We also spent time in group reflecting on how we listened and responded to each other.**

**Today we will begin our time of attending to spiritual guidance by entering the gospel narrative in John, chapter 1. I invite you to pray with me, asking for the guidance and help of the Spirit of God.**

*Prayer:* **Again, Lord God, you bring us together. We are seekers and learners, and we ask for your help as we join those early seekers and listen along with them. Open the eyes of our souls to see, and the ears of our hearts to hear, in the name of Jesus Christ. Amen.**

## MEDITATION (30 MINUTES)

*Practicing the Spiritual Discipline of Entering the Story*

Our gospel companion, John, invites us to enter into the story, to be present on the banks of the River Jordan. It is the day after Jesus has been baptized by John the Baptist.

Read this account from John 1:35-39 twice.

> The next day John again was standing with two of his disciples, and as he watched Jesus walk by, he exclaimed, "Look, here is the Lamb of God!" The two disciples heard him say this, and they followed Jesus. When Jesus turned and saw them following, he said to them, "What are you looking for?" They said to him, "Rabbi" (which translated means Teacher), "where are you staying?" He said to them, "Come and see." They came and saw where he was staying, and they remained with him that day.

After reading, continue with the following words, pausing at each caret sign (^) to allow time for encounter with and by the narrative:

**Close your eyes and imagine yourself standing on the bank of the Jordan River. ^ Feel the grass beneath your feet. Listen to the sound of the water. Feel the warmth of the sun on your face. ^ Notice John and two other men standing with him on the bank. Allow the sound of their conversation to enter your awareness. ^ Another man comes walking by: Jesus. ^ John the Baptist notices him first, and directs your attention to him: "Look, here is the Lamb of God!" ^**

**The Baptist's disciples begin following Jesus. You are also invited to go. As you begin walking up the bank and along the dirt road, Jesus turns and sees you following him. ^ He looks toward you, and asks, "What are you looking for?" What is your response? ^**

**One of the other men reply, "Rabbi, where are you staying?" Jesus again looks at you, and says, "Come and see." ^**

**Notice your response to Jesus. ^ As you are ready, be with Jesus now. ^ Stay with him. Get in touch with what you are looking for and bring your desires and longings to Jesus. Listen to his response to you. Simply be in his presence. ^**

*Discernment*
- What are you looking for? for your life and ministry? in this study and learning experience?
- In what ways did you find yourself being present to or resisting being Jesus?

GROUP REFLECTION (30 MINUTES)

*Leader:* We help another person to discern when we listen carefully without trying to formulate a reply. Listening asks that we simply hear the other person. We invite another's deeper reflection with open-ended questions such as:
- Can you tell more about _____?
- How was _____ for you?
- How did _____ feel for you? What kind of response did you sense was going on inside of you?

- As you think back to that time, what was God like for you?
- In what ways are you aware of God's presence in your life? When do you become aware of God being present?
- What does God seem to be asking of you?
- What is your response to God?

None of these questions elicits a yes or no answer. Instead, they invite further reflection, a deeper awareness. In this way we assist individuals to be present to themselves on a soul level.

Invite the group to form pairs and share their experiences of entering the narrative in John 1 or a wilderness time in their life. Each person spends ten minutes sharing that experience and being listened to by his or her partner.

SMALL-GROUP REFLECTION (30 MINUTES)

*Leader:* Reflect on how it felt to be the listener and on your experience of being listened to.

- What gets in the way or blocks your listening? sharing?
- What assists you to be present to the other, to be open and hospitable in your listening?
- What helps you to share your story when listened to?

CLOSURE (20 MINUTES)

Begin making plans for a group retreat. Guidance for retreat planning and content is given in chapter 8.

Our assignment for next time will be to read chapter 5, "Learning to Follow Jesus." Take time to respond prayerfully to the Reflection sections in this chapter and to journal your responses. Bring your Bibles, a copy of the book, and your journal at our next meeting. Two "Dialogues with Jesus" may be accessed on the Internet at www.upperroom.org/dialogues. These two conversations (numbers 1 and 2) offer a window into how Jesus related to persons from different backgrounds and understandings.

As we close, we'll pray for each other in pairs.

# Learning to Follow Jesus

*Blessed are the merciful, for they will receive mercy.*
*—Matthew 5:7*

Soon after their first encounter with Jesus at the River Jordan near Bethany, Simon, Andrew, James, and John return to their homes on the north shore of the Sea of Galilee. Their journey takes them some eighty miles by foot if they follow the ancient trade routes along with Roman roads built to facilitate military movement. These men, fishermen along with their fathers, are as much at home in a boat on the lake as they are eating at table with their families in Bethsaida (House of Fish) and Capernaum, another fishing town and the location of a significant Roman military presence. They are also disciples of John the Baptist, and during their time with John he has directed their attention to Jesus. They have met the messiah, the one whom they believed would restore the nation of Israel. This hope warms their hearts and excites their minds as these men settle back into the only work they know—casting nets into the rich fishing beds in this friendly but sometimes stormy sea.

Simon Peter invites us to walk into the gospel narrative and to join them as they return to work. Read Mark 1:14-20 prayerfully. Barefoot, we wade into the stony shallows of the lake and stand knee-deep in the clear fresh water, watching as the fishermen throw great circles of cast nets out onto the surface and wait as the nets sink into the sea.

It is to Capernaum that Jesus also comes. John the Baptist has been arrested and imprisoned by Herod, and Jesus withdraws to Galilee in the north. Rather than settling in the village where he played, learned, and lived from childhood until adulthood, Jesus leaves Nazareth and makes his home in Capernaum by the sea, in the territory of Zebulun and Naphtali, so that what the prophet Isaiah had spoken might be fulfilled:

> Land of Zebulun, land of Naphtali, on the road by the sea, across the Jordan, Galilee of the Gentiles—the people who sat in darkness have seen a great light, and for those who sat in the region and shadow of death light has dawned (Matt. 4:15-16).

In Jesus, God comes among us, walking the shores of this lake, "proclaiming the good news of God, and saying, 'The time is fulfilled, and the kingdom of God has come near; repent, and believe in the good news'" (Mark 1:14-15).

As we watch the disciples fishing and wait for them to draw in the cast nets, we become aware that we are not alone. Jesus joins us as we wait and watch. In such quiet ways God comes alongside us, in the daily work, our common routine. We are often unaware of this divine presence, even as these disciples are unaware that this is the Son of God standing knee-deep in the lake alongside them. However, they have begun to pin their hopes on Jesus as the messiah. So when he says, "Follow me and I will make you fish for people," they are ready to give him their loyalty. They have been waiting for this one who would save them and their people.

These fishermen do not fully understand the meaning of Jesus' call. A few centuries later, Francis of Assisi responds to God's call to repair the church by collecting stones to restore church buildings. Only in time, as Francis continues to listen to God's guidance, does he realize the Lord is calling him to heal the body of Christ: that was the "church" in need of repair. In the same way, these early disciples begin following Jesus, expecting him to be a political and military liberator. Gradually they learn the meaning of his call to set people free from all levels of oppression, and they appreciate the peace he brings through self-giving.

## Learning to Listen As We Follow

What does Jesus have in mind when he says, "Follow me"? What does fishing for people look like? And how does the "I will make you . . ." happen? Simon Peter remembers learning to follow Jesus. Luke also comes alongside and shares the experience of the other disciples. Read Mark 1:21-39 and Luke 4:31-44 prayerfully.

On the evening of the sabbath, a great crowd gathers around the door of Simon's house. A man possessed by a demon has been healed in the local synagogue, and Simon's mother-in-law also has been healed. People are bringing others who seek relief from demonic oppression and healing from illness. Simon Peter remembers watching as Jesus cured those who were sick and cast out demons. The question that persons in the synagogue kept asking rings in his ears: "What is this? . . . He commands even the unclean spirits, and they obey him" (Mark 1:27).

At sunrise the next day the crowd returns to Simon's door, asking for Jesus, bringing others for healing and help. But Jesus is nowhere to be found—neither in the house nor along the beach. The disciples take us with them as they climb up into the hills around the lake. While it was still dark Jesus had arisen and gone out to this deserted place to pray. Simon doesn't wait for Jesus to end his prayer; he blurts out, "Everyone is searching for you," and goes on to tell Jesus about the many people at the door of his house. As he speaks, the crowd also begins joining us on the mountainside, asking Jesus to come back into town.

Jesus addresses the people with the simple authority we heard when he taught in the synagogue the previous morning: "I must proclaim the good news of the kingdom of God to the other cities also; for I was sent for this purpose" (Luke 4:43). Then he turns toward our companions and says, "Let us go on to the neighboring towns, so that I may proclaim the message there also" (Mark 1:38). In the solitude of this deserted place, Jesus has drawn apart from the many voices that clamor for his attention.

CHAPTER 5

# BEING SHAPED AND TRANSFORMED:
## "I WILL MAKE YOU . . ."

As we follow Jesus along the mountain path, we realize we are learning what choosing to follow is about: Jesus is also a follower but not of the crowd or of popular opinion. Jesus knows how to listen to God. Other voices are loud, many, and insistent: "Everyone is searching for you!" We would naturally expect Jesus to return to the city forthwith and minister to the crowd waiting outside Peter's front door. After all, that is what all the people are asking for. We would allow their voices to control our decision making.

The call to follow Jesus means learning to listen as *he* listens. In the solitude of the mountain, Jesus is alone with God. Here Jesus can listen for God's voice, the voice of the One who sent him into our world. "The words that I say to you I do not speak on my own; but the Father who dwells in me does his works" (John 14:10). In this solitary place we are also called to listen and to discern the voices that control and direct our lives. Who is in charge? Which kingdom rules? Here we encounter the transformational work of God in our lives.

I remember my first experience of listening during a silent retreat. As I sat at the dining table eating lunch in silence, I became aware of how much I used talking as a way of coping with anxiety, especially if I did not know the other persons at table. Eye contact felt uncomfortable, so I decided to look out the window at the far end of the room. A small, sheltered flower garden was there, bordered by a long stone wall. Since I could not see much of the flower garden, I focused on the wall. There it stood: silent, still. And here I sat, uncomfortable, self-conscious. My coping mechanism of asking questions of others, learning to know them, listening to their stories, had been stripped away by the rule of silence. I felt angry, and inside myself I wanted to beat on that wall. It became an icon for my frustration with silence. After a while my anger subsided and I just sat, thinking a little about what lay beyond the wall: the home of the retreat center directors. The thought occurred to me that the wall served a purpose for them; it gave them some privacy and space within this expanse of retreat acreage with all its responsibilities. Behind the wall they could retreat, find solitude, and be restored.

Quite suddenly but just as quietly, I saw how silence is also a wall, offering privacy and space within the expanse of pastoral work and its responsibilities. I had moved beyond the resistance of my fear and frustration and entered the field of silence. Here I was invited to take off my pastoral hat, to allow myself to be cared for. Here I would be shepherded and pastored by God. Here I could rest and be restored.

## REFLECTION

All through the scriptures we find God drawing people into wilderness and solitude. In such deserted places we are relieved of our schedules and responsibilities, stripped of what we do not need. No radio, cell phone, computer, books, papers to process, projects to do, tapes to listen to. "The desert . . . lacks everything except the opportunity to know God."[1]

Read Mark 1:35. Jesus invites us to follow him into such quiet places. As you read the questions, spend the suggested time in silent thought.

- Where is your place of solitude? (1 minute)
- Where do you go in order to be alone with God? (2 minutes)
- In the solitary place we learn the spiritual discipline of silence— simply being in God's presence, listening. As you listen, notice the voices that enter your awareness. (1 minute)
- What response, if any, do the voices seem to invite or demand? (1 minute)
- Listen now to Jesus speaking to you: "I am the good shepherd. The sheep hear my voice. I call my own sheep by name and lead them out. My sheep follow me because they know my voice. Follow me." (15 minutes of silent listening)

*Discernment.* As you respond to the invitation to solitude, what do you become aware of within your self? What movement (toward the invitation) or countermovement (resistance to solitude) do you experience? How do you respond to Jesus' call? Do you resist? What invitation do you sense within this time of listening and solitude?

CHAPTER 5

# BEING SHAPED AND TRANSFORMED:
## "I WILL MAKE YOU FISH FOR PEOPLE."

While we are doing the work of God we also discover that we *are* the work of God. God is at work in us. This is what the disciples discover as they leave their nets and boats to follow Jesus. And this is what they invite us to discover as we walk alongside them.

Simon Peter draws our attention now to the people who come to Jesus and those whom Jesus seeks out, inviting us to enter the gospel narrative in Mark 1:40–3:6. We will become aware of the religious leaders of the day. Their lives are steeped in a long tradition of following the Mosaic law; they also are listening, watching, and asking questions about Jesus. At the heart of their observance of the Law lies the need to be righteous and thus acceptable before God. The Pharisees place a great deal of emphasis on gaining righteousness by separating themselves from people whom they consider unclean, even refusing to eat with anyone who does not observe certain laws and traditions. Some persons are judged untouchable and became social outcasts, creating a rift within the community of Israel.

Jesus surprises everyone as he moves with compassion into this painful fracture, offering the healing invitation of the kingdom, fishing for people. He wades into this restless sea, casting the net wide, announcing God's love and presence. He offers us spiritual direction, challenging our tidy religious and social rules in his response to a leper who approaches, kneels before him, and says, "If you choose, you can make me clean." Moved with pity (suffering with this man who suffers), Jesus stretches out his hand, touches him, and says, "I so choose. Be made clean!"

The Mosaic law forbade persons with leprosy from being present in their local community. Those with leprosy learned to stand at a distance, announcing their presence with the words, "Unclean! Unclean!" alerting others to pass at a distance. The blessing and comfort of touch was unknown to them. Jesus is both angry and full of compassion: angry because of the pain and the rift this man inhabits, full of pity because of this man's illness and his deep, inner loneliness. Healing needs to sink into the many layers of this man's life. Thus Jesus also offers pastoral guidance to assist people in welcoming this man back into community.

Jesus pays attention to the faith shown by a small group of persons who bring a paralytic for healing. Simon remembers their digging a hole through the roof of his house in order to make a way for their friend to get to Jesus. We begin to realize that when we bring others to God, God knows and sees our faith. Again in this incident, Jesus discerns need for a deeper healing and gives it. The paralyzed man receives the relief that accompanies forgiveness along with the healing of his body.

At this point we encounter criticism directed at Jesus' audacity to forgive sins. Some religious leaders are present, and we hear Jesus inviting these scribes to discern the cause of their own paralysis of faith when he asks, "Why do you raise such questions in your hearts?" When we move too quickly toward rational questioning and debate in the presence of God's love, healing, and forgiveness, we need to ask ourselves what we are avoiding and what prevents us from reaching across the gap.

Jesus stands in another rift within the politics of society when he calls Levi, a tax collector who works in the customs office along the shores of Capernaum, to follow him. Shock waves stir within the minds of the Zealots who were also beginning to accompany Jesus. Violently opposed to any foreign power intruding into the life of their nation, these freedom fighters despise anyone who betrays national loyalty, especially those who collect taxes from the Jews to pay to the Romans. In response to the scribes and Pharisees who ask why Jesus accepts Levi's invitation to dinner—along with other sinners—Jesus explains whom God invites: "Those who are well have no need of a physician, but those who are sick; I have come to call not the righteous but sinners." Jesus directs our attention here to the new shape and the grace-filled hospitality of the kingdom. The new wine of the kingdom banquet, being poured out for all to drink, needs fresh wineskins. Our structures and spiritual disciplines are to serve the inbreaking of God's presence and work in the world.

Then comes the sabbath. Jesus declares this day a gift for people rather than a rigid set of rules and traditions. This sabbath gift becomes one of healing for a man with a withered hand as he worships in the synagogue. Jesus looks at the Pharisees with anger and asks, "Is it lawful to do good or to do harm on the sabbath, to save life or to kill?" He grieves at their hardness of heart—the locus of what truly defiles and distorts our seeing, our hearing, our understanding, and our actions. With compassion he turns to the man and says, "Stretch out your hand." When they see his hand restored to health, the Pharisees walk out of the synagogue and conspire with the Herodians to destroy Jesus.[2]

> Throughout all of Scripture, the true prophet sides with the poor. The false prophet, on the other hand, bolsters the comfort and security of the powerful. The true prophet points out the divine presence and power, always in the context of community, and with a view toward judgment that moves the people toward justice. . . . The links with spiritual direction are clear. Both prophet and spiritual director stand in a position of recognizing and mediating God's perspective, proclaiming God's ways.[3]

## REFLECTION

Did a passage in the narrative particularly draw your attention? Stay with this passage, listening, observing, being present with the people in the text and with Jesus.

- What rifts are you aware of within the place or community where you minister?
- What people are difficult for you to envision being present to? Are there persons or groups you tend to avoid?
- Do you recall being drawn to reach out to someone but not acting out of fear of others' criticism?
- What response emerges within you when you are criticized?
- Who assists you to discern the voice and leading of God in your life and ministry?
- What questions arise in your heart as you reflect on following Jesus and being shaped by him for the invitational ministry of companioning persons into the kingdom?

# Attending to Spiritual Guidance

## GATHERING AND SETTLING IN (15 MINUTES)

Discuss any further arrangements for date, place, persons assisting, and other details for the group's retreat.

*Leader:* **During our last time together, we practiced the spiritual discipline of entering the gospel narrative, coming alongside John the Baptist and the early followers of Jesus. We paid attention to how Jesus asks them and us, "What are you looking for?" and then invites us, "Come and see." We are learning to help one another discern as we listen carefully, deeply, and then reflect on how the work of listening is going for each of us.**

## MEDITATION (30 MINUTES)

**For our opening meditation, we are invited into solitude and listening. After an opening prayer, I will be using the guidance for the preceding Reflection sections on pages 77 and 80. We will spend twenty minutes in the guided meditation and silence, followed by ten minutes of sharing our experience of silence and listening with a partner. You will be using your responses to the discernment questions on page 80 to assist you in sharing with one another.**

*Prayer:* **Loving and listening God, you who call us into the wilderness to be with you, and to listen, help us now by your Spirit as we open our attention to your presence. Help us to hear you, in Jesus' name. Amen.**

Read Mark 1:32-39. Then, using the Reflection on page 77, guide the group in this time of silent listening, pausing where indicated. Allow about five minutes for the guided meditation followed by fifteen minutes of silence.

*Being Present to Each Other One-on-One* (10 minutes). **Working in pairs, take turns listening to each other (five minutes each) as you share your experience of silence and your responses to the discernment questions on page 80.**

## SMALL-GROUP REFLECTION (30 MINUTES)

*Leader:* Let's take time to reflect on how it felt to be the listener and on our experiences of being listened to.

- How did it go for you?
- What kind of roles do you find yourself moving into as you listen: teacher? preacher? theologian? let-me-tell-you-my-story responder? fixer?
- What seems to trigger one or more of these responses in you?
- What assists you to be present to the other, to be open and hospitable in your listening?
- In what ways are you aware of your being more present and focused in your listening?

## SMALL-GROUP DISCUSSION (35 MINUTES)

- In what ways are you discovering what following Jesus is about in your life and ministry?
- How are you becoming aware of Jesus at work, "making you"— shaping and transforming you as you learn to hear Jesus' call to follow him in all of life?
- What kinds of "rifts" have you encountered as you follow?
- What are the challenges you face: fear, criticism, misunderstanding, rejection?
- How do the responses of Jesus shape and inform your response?

## CLOSURE (10 MINUTES)

Today we attended to the call of Jesus: "Follow me, and I will make you fish for people." We are learning that following Jesus calls us to listen, to be with God, and to learn the spiritual discipline of solitude and silence. This being with God empowers us to colabor with Jesus as he invites all kinds of persons into the kingdom of God. We continue to learn how to listen to each other.

In preparation for our next session, read chapter 6, "Going Deeper: Learning to Be with Jesus." Take time to respond to the Reflection sections in this chapter and to journal your responses.

Close in prayer. Bring into God's presence those individuals and groups who are caught in the painful rifts in society—in your own spheres of ministry, in the community, in the nation, and in the world.

# Chapter 6

# Going Deeper: Learning to Be with Jesus

*Blessed are the poor in spirit, for theirs is
the kingdom of God.—Matthew 5:8*

When Jesus calls us to follow him, we may not be aware of the images
we have of God or Jesus. Hans Denck, a thoughtful and insightful spiritual writer during the Reformation, was aware of how our perception of
God can color and shape our thinking and responses. Denck discerned
that some persons constantly need to run from God and hide, frightened
of what God might do to them. Mim, the seminary student who saw
God as an ogre, could identify with Denck's spiritual guidance. "For since
you are a poor little plant and [God] an enormous stone you are always
anxious that he will crush you if you hold still for him. . . ."[1] Denck invites
us to hold still, for God comes to us gently. Jesus is the Lamb of God
who takes away the sin of the world.

Simon Peter remembers his own need to hide from God. He asks
us to join him on the day that Jesus leaves his house to walk to the seashore

nearby. Listen prayerfully to his experience recorded in Mark 3:7-12 and Luke 5:1-11.

The day begins like many other days. No matter where Jesus goes, a crowd seems to gather. Simon does not recall what Jesus taught the multitude that day, but he does remember Jesus' asking to use his boat as a place to sit while teaching. Later that boat becomes as a place for personal spiritual direction.

## BEING WITH JESUS ON THE LAKE

When he had finished speaking, he said to Simon, "Put out into the deep water and let down your nets for a catch." Simon answered, "Master, we have worked all night long but have caught nothing. Yet if you say so, I will let down the nets." When they had done this they caught so many fish that their nets were beginning to break. So they signaled their partners in the other boat to come and help them. And they came and filled both boats, so that they began to sink. But when Simon Peter saw it, he fell down at Jesus' knees, saying, "Go away from me, Lord, for I am a sinful man!" For he and all who were with him were amazed at the catch of fish that they had taken. . . . Then Jesus said to Simon, "Do not be afraid; from now on you will be catching people" (Luke 5:4-10).

Simon sees Jesus' divine power produce the miraculous catch of fish, and suddenly he is engulfed by fear. He feels unable, unclean, unacceptable in the presence of this holy One in his boat. He falls down at Jesus' knees and begs him to leave. Momentarily Simon has forgotten similar encounters that Isaiah and Jeremiah had with Yahweh. Isaiah laments, "Woe is me! I am lost, for I am a man of unclean lips, . . . yet my eyes have seen . . . the LORD of hosts!" (Isa 6:5). Jeremiah remonstrates about himself: "Ah, Lord GOD! Truly I do not know how to speak, for I am only a boy" (Jer. 1:6). Isaiah dreads what will happen to him; Jeremiah is dismayed at his inadequacy; and Simon wants Jesus out of his life. That would solve Simon's problem. He would no longer have to feel afraid, weak, and sinful in the presence of this One who knew more about the lake and fish than he did.

Spiritual director and psychiatrist Gerald May speaks of self-identifying spiritual experiences which may feel "too revealing. They can easily provide glimpses of one's repressed desires. . . . and often one would rather not be made aware of them."[2]

The male false self tends toward desire to be strong and able. In Western society a dominant philosophy still holds that "big boys don't cry." The strong man shows no emotion. A seminary student remembers playing football in high school: "We practiced every day after school for hours. I began to get the message after a week or two. If it hurts, suck it up: no pain, no gain. Throwing my body on the ground as part of the practice drill to save the ball or make a tackle was good; it would toughen me up, make me strong for the team, and bring out the man in me. No matter how bruised or sore my body felt later that night and the next day, we would begin pounding our bodies all over again during practice. This was all so that we could win the game and make a name for our school's team." The more sensitive, less competitive male finds himself struggling with his sense of self: "What if I'm not a jock? Then who am I?"

To Peter's surprise, Jesus does not leave. Jesus looks at him and says, "Don't be afraid. From now on you will be catching people." This is how God comes. Rather than condemnation or abandonment, Isaiah, Jeremiah, and Simon Peter hear God's invitation to stay close and to colabor with God in the world.[3]

The kingdom of God comes and meets us where we are. We are invited to be still, to hear God's call to turn from fear of condemnation for who we are and what we have done, and to know we are accepted where we are.

## REFLECTION

*Practicing the Spiritual Discipline of Entering the Narrative*

*Preparation.* Pray for the Holy Spirit to help you see and hear with your soul. Read the narrative in Luke 5:1-11 twice, slowly.

*Entering.* As you walk into the scene in the gospel narrative, use your senses. Feel the stones on the beach beneath your feet. See the great crowd gathered close to the shore. Feel the warmth of the sun on your face and back and the lake breeze on your face. Smell the nets drying in the sun. Look around you and notice where you choose to sit in the boat as Jesus tells Simon to "put out into the deep water." Hear the splash of the waves against the sides of the boat. Finally the boat comes to the deep waters of the lake.

Listen as Jesus tells Peter to let down his nets. Now Jesus turns to you and invites you to let down your net into the deep. How do you respond?

What is in your net as you pull it to the surface? How do you feel as you sort through what is there in the presence of Jesus? What do you want to say—or not want to say—to Jesus?

Listen to Jesus' words to you: "Do not be afraid. From now on you will be catching people." Be with Jesus in conversation and then in simple silence as you sit in the boat together.

*Discernment.* Where did you sit in the boat in relation to Simon? to Jesus? What responses emerged as Jesus invited you to let down your net into the deep? as you pulled it up? as you noticed what was in it?

What do you notice about your fears? How do you respond when Jesus tells you not to be afraid? How do you respond to his call to the invitational ministry of companioning people into the kingdom?

---

## FEAR AND AVOIDANCE OF GOD

Deep within our beings we are fearful people. We fear being harmed, dying, and hence fear fire, drowning, falling, and a host of events that could harm or kill us. In response, we create laws that protect our safety and arrange our lives in ways that foster security. Stoplights at intersections, double yellow lines, caution signs, and speed limits all speak of a reverence for life, as well as our desire to protect ourselves from the fear of being harmed.

We experience another kind of fear, an internal dread in the face of rejection, abandonment, or condemnation. From birth, children need to know they are wanted, loved, safe, and accepted. Without these gifts of loving presence and care from parents and caregivers, a painful and empty place can settle into the soul of the child, resulting in all kinds of behaviors—often addictive—in an attempt to fill the vacuum.

However, even persons who grow up with caring, good parents and caregivers may experience this dread and fear of rejection and loss. To some extent we all do. Ever since Eden all humankind has been living at a lonely distance from God, self, others, and creation. Each of us experiences this existential loneliness that only God can remedy.

As a child I used to walk outside at night to gaze up at the stars. There in the quiet mystery and beauty I would sometimes get in touch with a knowledge that all people would one day appear before God. Once that thought emerged in my soul, however, another thought followed. I would also be required to appear. And God would see me as dirty and unacceptable and would throw me out of heaven. This fearful scenario filled me with dread and fear which caused me to abruptly stop thinking about it. My reasoning? Then I would not feel the fear. Separation and distance are two aspects of death, physical death being the separation of the soul from the body. Into these interior spaces of dread, loneliness, loss, and fear of eternal abandonment Jesus speaks good news.

At times in our travels through the Gospels we will hear Jesus calling his followers "children" or "little ones." Simon, even though he ran a fishing business, was still a child in his faith response. "Go away from me, Lord, for I am a sinful man!" Just as I reasoned childishly about avoiding certain thoughts, Simon believed that if Jesus left, his problem would disappear. The ministry of spiritual direction helps us to uncover our negative and distorted images of God; we also come to see and name our fear and avoidance. Just as Simon needed time and the patient companioning of Jesus to confess his weakness and lack of loyalty to Jesus, I needed time to come to know God's gracious acceptance of me just as I am.

Jesus comes to us where we are, with our fears and childlike ways of hiding, and speaks reassurance. "Don't be afraid. I am here, with you. I invite you to stay with me. I am here to show you what God is like, and to bring the good news of God's love and acceptance" (John 14:9, AP).

## LEARNING TO BE WITH JESUS: RETREAT ON THE MOUNTAIN

We are invited into retreat. Our gospel companions lead us up a mountain—a deserted place away from the crowd, the work of ministry, all that absorbs our attention and often clutters our perspective.

Simon recalls that early in his ministry, Jesus invited all those who were following him to enter into a rhythm of life and ministry:

- to come
- to be with
- and to be sent out.

We tend to focus on the being sent out into all the world of Mark 16 and Matthew 28. But Jesus includes all three movements in the life of his followers: turning aside from daily activity to come to Jesus, learning to be with him, and then responding as Jesus companions and directs his disciples on both an inward and outward journey. To enter fully into this time of retreat, invite the Spirit of God to help you see and hear with the eyes and ears of your heart. Read the narrative from Mark 3:13-19 slowly, prayerfully.

> Jesus went up the mountain
> and called to him those whom he wanted,
> and they came to him.
> And he appointed twelve . . .
> to be with him,
> and to be sent out
> to proclaim the message, and to have authority to cast out
> demons, [and to heal (see Mark 6:12-13; Matt.10:1)].
> So he appointed the twelve:
> Simon (to whom he gave the name Peter);
> James son of Zebedee and John the brother of James
> (to whom he gave the name Boanerges, that is, Sons of Thunder);
> . . . and Simon the Cananaean [who was called the Zealot (see
> Luke 6:15)].

### COMING

Jesus calls us to come. Our turning aside from the daily is response to his call. Congregations and search committees are beginning to re-vision the nature and content of ministry descriptions to include time and space for prayerful solitude.

## BEING WITH

> They came to him . . . to be with him (Mark 3:13-14).

This time with Jesus puts us in the place where we learn to stop and be present. While this sounds simple, we discover that this shift to "being with" is not always easy. Even though we are in retreat on the mountainside, the agenda of the previous twenty-four hours or week continues to sound its many voices and demands within our consciousness. We need to be patient. The work of the soul cannot be hurried.

It can be helpful to name whatever comes to mind, to visualize each thing, and then to lay it at the feet of Jesus there on the ground of the mountainside. For those who are not so visually oriented, write a list of what demands your attention, and then lay the list prayerfully in a safe place, offering its contents to God for safekeeping.

## BEING NAMED: THE INWARD JOURNEY

In the quiet of retreat Jesus names the disciples: "Simon (to whom he gave the name Peter); James son of Zebedee and John the brother of James (to whom he gave the name Boanerges, that is Sons of Thunder), . . . and Simon the Cananaean [who was called the Zealot (Luke 6:15)]." This is an inward naming that shapes the hearer. Jesus draws our attention to the "I will make you. . . ." We begin to know ourselves and to become aware of what is within.

Simon thinks he is a rock, a Peter. As he continues to share with us his own story and pilgrimage, Simon reveals how little he was aware of his own weaknesses and how much he avoided knowing. Jesus begins by giving him a strong nickname, thus assuring Simon of his potential in Jesus' sight, and invites Simon to continue to be known and named.

James and John also need guidance for their inner journey. Patiently, gently, and clearly, Jesus offers spiritual guidance to them, inviting them to begin owning and dealing with their anger response when confronted with certain situations. In the face of rejection these brothers would want to command fire to come down from heaven and consume those who would not accept them. Jesus wants to help them discern what spirit and attitude lurks within their souls.

Simon the Cananaean is invited to reflect on his beliefs as a Zealot and to get in touch with his hostile attitude toward certain people, including Levi (Matthew), the tax collector. Sometimes the people we are called to live and work with in ministry will arouse all kinds of negative reactions within us. Simon is called to confront these thoughts.

## BEING NAMED: THE OUTWARD JOURNEY

Our gifts and strengths are named. Now we receive direction for the invitational ministry of companioning others into the kingdom. "And he appointed twelve, whom he also named apostles, to be with him, and to be sent out to proclaim the message, and to have authority to cast out demons" and to heal (see Mark 6:12 and Matt.10:1). On the outward journey of being sent, our lives and our practice of ministry—no matter what our call and gifting—will bear the mark of Jesus' call to communicate the good news, to confront evil, and to be a presence for healing.

Throughout our gospel pilgrimage these early disciples will continue to direct our attention to Jesus who embodies God's presence and love in his being and doing. Jesus communicates good news, confronts the evil that blocks our learning and our responding to God's gracious invitation. Jesus brings healing into the painful rift in which we live.

### REFLECTION

Reflect on the rhythm to which Jesus calls his disciples—to come, to be with him, to respond. Then consider these questions:

- How is Jesus directing your attention concerning your rhythm of life, rest, prayerful solitude, and the work of ministry?
- What is being named within you as you wait in the presence of God?
- In what ways are you responding to God?

- In what ways are you resisting what God is naming and discerning within you?
- How would you describe your sense of outward naming, the call of God on your life to serve within the church? beyond the church?
- In what way does your ministry flow out of the gifts and graces God has given you?
- In what ways does your ministry bear the mark of Jesus' call to communicate good news (in word, in deed, in your way of being in the world around you)? to confront evil (in yourself, in the body of Christ, in the world)? to be a presence for healing?
- In what ways are you empowered to heal?

# Attending to Spiritual Guidance

## GATHERING AND SETTLING IN (15 MINUTES)

*Leader:* We began our last session of attending to spiritual guidance by practicing the spiritual discipline of silence and solitude. We also spent time discussing Jesus' call on our lives: "Follow me, and I will make you fish for people." What does it means to follow, to be made, and to companion people into the kingdom of God? We also reflected on the various divisions among people and the challenges we encounter as we minister to persons, no matter who they are and how society views them.

For our meditation today we will be entering the gospel narrative of Luke 5:1-11. After an opening prayer we will spend twenty minutes practicing the spiritual discipline and then have ten minutes for sharing our experience with a partner.

## MEDITATION (30 MINUTES)

*Prayer:* **Loving God, you invite us to go deeper with you and with ourselves. Help us by your Holy Spirit as we take our boat out into the deep waters. Open the eyes of our heart to see. In the name of Jesus, Amen.**

Using the guidance offered on pages 87–88, lead the group into the gospel narrative. (20 minutes) Share in pairs the experience of this prayer form, using questions offered in the Discernment section. (10 minutes)

## GROUP REFLECTION (1 HOUR)

Take fifty minutes to work through the section "Learning to Be with Jesus: Retreat on the Mountain," beginning on page 90. After some discussion of the scripture and chapter content, share with one another your responses to the Reflection section on pages 92–93. You may have journal entries to share here. Be hospitable and present as you listen to one another.

Take ten minutes now to reflect on how your listening is going. Share your learnings in group.

*Leader:* **What are you noticing regarding the presence of your own inner agenda as you listen? Does it tend to intrude itself into the way you listen, or are you able to simply notice it and stay in a clear and open space of hospitable listening, knowing that you can always address your own agenda later?**

## CLOSURE (15 MINUTES)

Our opening meditation took us out into the deeper waters of the lake and of our lives as we entered into the gospel narrative in Luke 5:1-11. The rest of our time we spent in group conversation about Jesus' call to be with him in retreat on the mountain: coming, being with, being named on the inward journey and for the outward journey. We also took a few minutes to reflect together on how our listening is going.

In preparation for our next session of attending to spiritual guidance, read chapter 7 in the book and the third "Dialogue with Jesus," accessible on the Web at www.upperroom.org/dialogues. Respond to the Reflection sections in chapter 7, and journal your responses.

For a closing prayer, pray for one another's sense of gifting, call, and ministry.

# Being Formed for Ministry

*Blessed are the pure in heart, for they will see God.*
*—Matthew 5:8*

As we gather again by the Sea of Galilee, Jesus begins teaching in parables—those stories that entice our imagination with color and content and invite our curiosity. He gathers the stuff of everyday life—soils and seeds, grain and rocks, lamps and baskets, yeast and bread—into the net of his storytelling. Simon Peter remembers Jesus sitting in one of his boats moored in the shallows of the sea, sharing the contents of this net of stories with the crowd gathered on the beach. Enter the narrative Simon Peter offers in Mark 4:1-34 and listen prayerfully.

## TENDING THE SOILS OF THE SOUL

This first parable tells a story about soils and seeds. In it Jesus mentions rocks and weeds that spoil the harvest and diminish the crop. However, Simon Peter remembers being asked to pay closer attention to the bookends Jesus places at each end of the parable: the first word, "Listen!" and the last statement, "Let anyone with ears to hear listen!" (Mark 4:3, 9). With these signals, the parable begins to reveal its deeper meaning: it concerns listening. Even though our gospel companions hear the parable, they do not understand its meaning. When alone with Jesus, they ask him about the parable. Placing ourselves alongside the disciples, we join this private meeting for spiritual guidance. Jesus looks around at us and says, "To you has been given the secret of the kingdom of God, but for those outside, everything comes in parables; . . . Do you not understand this parable? Then how will you understand all the parables?" (Mark 4:11, 13).

No, we don't understand the parable. Its meaning is hidden, a mystery. Jesus reassures us that "there is nothing hidden, except to be disclosed; nor is anything secret, except to come to light" (Mark 4:21; Luke 8:18). Meaning will be given as we pay attention to what we hear and how we listen. God desires to show us, to bring meaning to light. Our receptive listening opens us to the work of the Holy Spirit who reveals the mystery of the kingdom to us. Benedict, giving spiritual guidance in the sixth century, said, "Let us open our eyes to the light that comes from God, and our ears to the voice from heaven that every day calls out this charge: . . . *You that have ears to hear, listen to what the Spirit says to the churches* (Rev 2:7)."[1] Founder of the Benedictine Order, Benedict embraced the gospel as the order's guide and called persons to a close listening to scripture. The spiritual discipline *lectio divina* was central to the monks' lives and became a way of listening as they prayed the scriptures in their worship and while working. Benedict admonished members of the order to "listen readily to holy reading, and devote yourself often to prayer."[2]

Jesus knows that certain things prevent us from hearing and understanding with the heart (Matt. 13:15), and it is to those things he now draws our attention. He points first to surface listening and hardness of heart. In Jesus' day, the heart is not regarded as the seat of the emotions but as the interior of who we are as persons—our soul and source of being.[3] The hard heart, also described by the prophet Ezekiel as a heart of stone (Ezek.11:19) resists the "honkings" of God. The interior of who we are is enclosed and insulated against God. Jesus reveals that Satan can snatch away what God is saying to persons with hardened hearts.

Second, Jesus speaks of rocky ground. Persons hear and receive what is given them, but something blocks their attention. What God is saying neither sinks deep into the interior of their soul nor takes root within them. All kinds of agendas can get in the way of this rooting: fear of authority figures, a distorted image of God, discomfort with one's self-image and fear of God's seeing it, unhealed memories, false teaching, abuse—spiritual, emotional, or physical. When their Christian faith brings troubles and trials, these persons tend to get discouraged and withdraw. Some may turn back and no longer follow Christ.

Third, Jesus refers to the thorns. Here he points to the anxieties of the world, the lure of wealth, and the desires that push into our interior space, misdirecting our attention and choking off desire for God's voice and God's way. The free-market consumer economy of today dictates how we use our money and traps us in its anxious philosophy. The underlying assumption of always needing more things in order to be somebody taps into the desires of our false self. Attaining security and satisfaction replaces seeking God; in fact, people feel no need for God—other than regarding God or religion as one more thing to accumulate.

Finally, there is the good soil. Here the word is received and listened to carefully and deeply; it takes root within the soul, bearing fruit in all of one's life and work. Here an understanding is given as the Holy Spirit brings clarity and meaning. This gift of clearsightedness helps us recognize the false within ourselves and in the world. We are then free to see and embrace the good of God's ways.

Jesus, as a wise spiritual director, is encouraging us to pay attention to our heart, the interior of our being. He offers this parable as a map for the inward journey of the soul, designed to help us notice and recognize the soils we discover—within our own lives and the lives of others.

Abba Moses, a desert father of the fourth century, invited the same careful noticing as he called for all the secret places of the heart to be attended to. This ancient spiritual guide said to "cultivate the earth of our heart with the gospel plow," then what is harmful can be rooted out.[4]

## REFLECTION

How do you read and listen to scripture?

Day after day the women of Jesus' time made bread. Jesus had watched his mother, Mary, count the measures of flour, knead the yeast mixture into dough, wait for it to rise, and then bake the bread. His memory of the rhythmic mixing and kneading becomes a parable. Jesus says, "The kingdom of heaven is like yeast that a woman took and mixed in with three measures of flour until all of it was leavened" (Matt. 13:33). Jesus recognizes the power of ideas and truths we incorporate into our thinking and allow to shape our inward and outward lives. Jesus uses the metaphor again when he warns the disciples against the yeast—the narrow theology—of the Pharisees (Mark 8:15).

Meditation on scripture allows the truths and life-giving theology of God to gradually permeate and shape our life and being.

---

## TENDING OUR FEARS AND OUR FAITH

Our gospel companions call our attention now to those times when our obedience to Jesus places us in situations beyond our control. Listen prayerfully as you read Mark 4:35-41.

No matter what circumstances we find ourselves in, Jesus asks questions that invite us to probe more deeply into ourselves and discover the soils, rocks, and weeds within. In this narrative, Jesus asks our gospel companions about their fear and about their lack of faith. In turn he also asks us, "Why are you afraid? Have you still no faith?"

Before we respond to the second question, we need to answer the first: Why are you afraid? In light of the circumstances the disciples were in, we may wonder why Jesus asks the question at all. The waves were so high they were breaking over their boat, filling it with water. In the midst of this danger the disciples interpret Jesus' being asleep as an attitude of indifference: "Teacher, do you not care that we are perishing?" Behind this reaction is fear: fear of drowning but also the deeper fear of God's being distant and nonattentive to their needs. Here we encounter rocky soil. In the face of difficulty, the disciples lack a deep rootedness in the presence and care of God. Hence their question echoes the laments and complaints within the Hebrew prayer book, the Psalms: "Has God forgotten to be gracious? Has he in anger shut up his compassion?" (Ps. 77:9). "How long, O LORD? Will you forget me forever?" (Ps. 13:1).

In his insightful work in the psalms, Walter Brueggemann traces a pattern within the experience of those who prayed.[5] First, they are securely oriented, settled. Life makes sense and is safe enough. Second, often quite suddenly, they become painfully disoriented. We know how events in our lives threaten and disrupt our sense of safety and calm. Since September 11, 2001, most people in the United States experience heightened fear, a sense of the world's fragility and insecurity. The psalms offer us voice for our fears. The third movement is toward rest, reorientation. The psalms of lament within the Hebrew tradition are prayers of disorientation. They offer permission to voice complaint and need, and they provide words that give expression to whatever we are experiencing.

While a lament may be spoken out of a distorted perception of who God is and what God is about, it is made *to* God. Voicing the complaint offers a way of stepping back a little to see and to name what troubles our soul. In the naming we begin creating a space between ourselves and this disruptive chaos, a space hospitable to God's help. Thus we learn to wait—in the midst of trouble—for God. And God responds.

Fran, having served as minister in a church for a year, was finding it difficult to preach. "I usually enjoy preaching," she said one day in my office, "but now I think I dread it." She paused for a few moments. I asked, "Can you tell me about dread?" Fran began to describe her experience more fully: "I feel tight, anxious, even fearful as I enter the pulpit to speak." In time Fran realized she feared many persons in the congregation, especially their opinion of her sermons. "I don't think they like my preaching," she lamented.

I invited her to see Jesus coming into the sanctuary of the church as the congregation was sitting in the pews and to notice what he might do or say. At first Fran felt intimidated in the presence of the gathered congregation, but as she watched Jesus first stand silently at the back of the church, then walk up the center aisle to the communion table, she began to notice a change in how the people looked, especially those who were most resistant to the preaching. Rather than appearing large and overpowering, these persons looked needy, disabled, and grieving. Several were bandaged; one leaned on crutches as he walked with difficulty to the communion table. All appeared sad, lonely, and in need of care. Fran found herself surprised and consoled as she saw Jesus offering bread and wine to each one. Some partook, some hesitated. But Jesus waited patiently and kindly.

Fran discovered she could see these persons in a new way, and her anxiety began to fade. In time she was enabled to envision addressing the deeper and more hidden need within the life of the congregation. She was experiencing the response God brings, which leads us into the third movement: the experience of being surprisingly reoriented. We discover, like Fran, that God comes to us in our desolation offering comfort and helping us see the situation with new eyes.

For the disciples, this new way of seeing opens them to wonder and reflection. They ask one another, "Who then is this, that even the wind and the sea obey him?" Their question signals the interior movement of the Holy Spirit, pulling at the door of their souls so that they may receive who Jesus is and what he can do. They are being invited toward faith and rootedness.

While our faith may seem small and inadequate to deal with what blocks our trust, God invites us to know and name our fears. Facing our fears is a stepping stone to greater faith.

## REFLECTION

Listen to Jesus asking, "Why are you afraid?" Prayerfully and honestly look into your life, paying attention to those times when you are fearful. Then wait and pause to ask yourself, Why am I afraid? What seems to happen to your sense of faith and trust when you are afraid?

As you get in touch with the fear, feel it, sit with it. How do you react? How do you pray or not pray? Where does God seem to be? What kind of complaint or lament would express how you feel, give words to your experience? The following psalms may be helpful: Psalm 6; 10; 12; 13; 16; 22; 31; 38; 55; 61; 64; 69; 77; and 86.

———◦◉◦———

## TENDING THE SHAPE OF OUR MINISTRY

Before sending the disciples out, Jesus invites them to be with him in Nazareth, the town where he grew up and where Mary and his brothers and sisters still live. As was his custom, Jesus goes to the synagogue on the sabbath day. Simon Peter draws us into the narrative in Mark 6:1-6. Listen prayerfully to his account, along with Luke's in Luke 4:16-21.

When the time comes for reading from one of the prophets, Jesus stands, and the scroll of Isaiah is given to him to read. Our companions remember waiting, watching as Jesus unrolls the scroll, finds a certain passage, and then reads:

> The Spirit of the Lord is upon me,
>   because he has anointed me
>     to bring good news to the poor.
> He has sent me to proclaim release to the captives
>   and recovery of sight to the blind,
>     to let the oppressed go free,
> to proclaim the year of the Lord's favor
> (Luke 4:18-19; see Isa. 61:1-2).

Jesus then rolls up the scroll, gives it back to the attendant, and sits down in one of the chairs facing the congregation, indicating that he is about to speak. Into the expectant hush of attention Jesus speaks good news: "Today this scripture has been fulfilled in your hearing." Now is the time of God's gracious freedom giving! Jesus has given the people and our gospel companions a description of what his ministry is about and who empowers him to do the tasks of ministry.

*To bring good news to the poor.* The literal meaning of the word translated "poor" is "begging"—those who beg. The meaning includes persons who expect little or nothing from the circumstances of their lives and recognize their dependence on God.

*To proclaim release to the captives and recovery of sight to the blind.* This release builds on the custom of the year of jubilee when persons who have been sold into slavery because of economic hardship are freed, and property that has changed hands returns to its original owner. In this way God reminds the people that "the land is mine; with me you are but aliens and tenants" (Lev. 25:23). Jesus' coming also means freedom for all who are in some kind of slavery, including slavery to sin (John 8:34). Recovery of sight to the blind includes healing for every type of blindness, including physical blindness and spiritual blindness (Mark 8:18, 22-25).

*To let the oppressed go free.* Here Jesus speaks freedom to persons who are oppressed, downtrodden, and broken religiously and socially—those held hostage by the painful fracture within society.

## BEING SENT OUT

The disciples remember being with Jesus in the cities and villages of Galilee as he continues to teach in the synagogues, proclaim the good news of the kingdom, and cure disease and sickness. Crowds gather around him. Multitudes follow him.

Matthew (also called Levi) knows all about crowds. He has watched people stand in line at the customs booth, waiting to pay their import tax. But *his* view of the crowds and *Jesus'* view of the multitude are two different things. It dawns on Matthew that the same hospitality Jesus extended to all who gathered at his house in Capernaum is extended to the multitude. Jesus has compassion for the crowd because they are harassed and helpless, like sheep without a shepherd. They are captive, oppressed, blind—with no one to guide them. This same compassion moves Jesus to invite the prayerful attention of those who follow him.

Matthew draws us aside now and invites our prayerful attention as we hear Jesus offer spiritual guidance and call us to prayer. Jesus says to his disciples, "The harvest is plentiful, but the laborers are few; therefore ask the Lord of the harvest to send out laborers into his harvest" (Matt. 9:35-38). This is God's field and God's work, and God gives the harvest. We are invited to colabor with God.

In the last few years denominational leaders have been keenly aware of the need for people to replace those pastors and persons in ministry who will retire within the next decade or two. Just as Jesus invites persons to follow him, to observe how he does the work of ministry, and to learn a rhythm of engagement and rest, those in ministry today can tap others to come alongside and observe. Just as Jesus begins the work of discerning the gifts, strengths, and places for growth in his followers, persons in ministry today can invite the next generation of pastors and leaders to prayerfully discern their gifts and sense of call.

The disciples enter into prayer, asking God to send laborers out into the harvest; they recognize the call of God on their own lives. They begin seeing people as Jesus does. Now Jesus calls these followers of his—first twelve and then seventy (Mark 6:7; Luke 10:1)—to come and be with him in preparation for going out. As we gather along with them, Jesus also addresses us. Listen prayerfully as Simon Peter, Matthew, and Luke companion us in the gospel narrative in Mark 6:7-13; Matthew 10; and Luke 9:1-6; 10:1-12.

Jesus is giving guidance for ministry: "As you go, proclaim the good news, 'The kingdom of heaven has come near.' Now is the time that God's rule is beginning." They are to take little with them and so be dependent on the hospitality of those who receive them into their homes while on the road.

Jesus does not overlook the possibility of opposition and rejection. Already the disciples have heard the criticism of the scribes and Pharisees and accusations that Jesus is out of his mind and demon-possessed. Matthew remembers Jesus' telling them that they can expect to be treated in the same way: "If they have called the master of the house Beelzebul, how much more will they malign those of his household!" (Matt. 10:25). Simon Peter remembers other forms of resistance to Jesus' ministry. When Jesus freed a man from the destructive power of a legion of demons and restored him to his family and community, some in the community became frightened and asked Jesus to leave. As Jesus entered the house of Jairus to heal his daughter, the mourners who had gathered mocked him and laughed. Even Jesus' family had sought to restrain him from doing further ministry. Resistance and rejection would be the disciples' experience also.

The time to leave arrives, and the disciples go on their way. What they have received free of charge from Jesus they offer freely to others: the good news of God's kingdom and an invitation for all to turn and enter; healing and relief to many who are sick (Matt.10:1 and Mark 6:12-13); and confrontation of evil spirits. The work of Jesus now becomes their work.

## REFLECTION

You are invited to spend time in prayerful solitude reflecting on your experience of this chapter in reference to your own life and ministry:

- In what ways does your work of ministry reflect the ministry description Jesus announces in Luke 4? in Mark 6 and Matthew 10—to proclaim the good news of the kingdom, to be a presence for healing, and to confront evil?
- In what ways does it differ?
- In what ways are you empowered for ministry?
- How do you respond to misunderstanding or rejection? In what ways do you sense God is present for you in such times?
- Think about fear and trust, being self-sufficient, and being dependent on God. Where do you sense your faith is strained? growing?
- How do you listen to God? to scripture? tend the soils of your heart?
- In what areas could you grow in faith and healthy dependency?
- In what ways do you give yourself freedom to lament?
- Who listens to you?
- How do you bring these matters into your prayer and presence for God?

# Attending to Spiritual Guidance

## GATHERING AND SETTLING IN (10 MINUTES)

Make any final arrangements for the retreat (if you are planning to work with chapter 8 in retreat format).

*Leader:* **In our last session we practiced the spiritual discipline of entering the narrative in Luke 5, learning to hear Jesus' call to go into the deeper waters of our lives. We also had group conversation about Jesus' call to be with him in retreat on the mountain: coming, being with, being named—on the inward journey and for the outward journey. And we spent a few minutes reflecting on how our listening is progressing.**

**In our meditation today we will hear Jesus' call to pay attention to how we listen.**

## MEDITATION (30 MINUTES)

**Jesus invites us to pay attention to how we listen. In this way we are being receptive to the work of the Holy Spirit who is tending the soils of our soul. The spiritual discipline *lectio divina* continues to help us listen on a deeper, soul level.**

*Prayer.* **Spirit of God, help us as we read and listen. Open the eyes and ears of our soul to see and to hear. In the name of Jesus, Amen.**

*Reading.* **Together, slowly read the following passages from Mark 4:21-25a and Luke 8:18 aloud twice. During the second reading, individuals may stop reading with the group when a phrase or word draws their attention. Persons stay with their word or phrase; they need not continue reading the whole passage as the leader finishes.**

> [Jesus] said to [the disciples], "Is a lamp brought in to be put under the bushel basket, or under the bed, and not on the lampstand? For there is nothing hidden, except to be disclosed; nor is anything secret, except to come to light. Let anyone with ears to hear listen!" And

he said to them, "Pay attention to what you hear; the measure you give will be the measure you get, and still more will be given you. For to those who have, more will be given."

Then pay attention to how you listen.

*Meditation.* Meditate on the word or phrase that captured your attention; be receptive to its content. Allow the meaning to break open to you.

*Prayer.* Respond to God in prayer, talking to God about what you are discovering as the word begins to read your life and to work the soils of your soul.

*Contemplation.* Be with God—in quiet rest, appreciation, presence. If your mind wanders, repeat the word you have been given as a way of remaining attentive and open to God's presence.

*Discernment*
- In what ways are you listening not only with your mind but also on a deeper level as the word enters the field of your heart?
- What seems to kidnap your attention?
- How do you respond to such kidnapping?
- What helps you return to prayerful presence?
- In what way is this word reading your life and tending the soils of your soul?

## GROUP REFLECTION (1 HOUR 10 MINUTES)

*Leader:* What are you noticing about your listening as you do the work of pastoral care and spiritual guidance in ministry? What has stayed the same for you? What is changing? (15 minutes)

In preparation for this session we were invited to read chapter 7 and to give prayerful consideration to the chapter content, to our own life, and to the shape of our ministry. Working in groups of three or four, share your journal responses to the Reflection section at the end of the chapter. (35 minutes)

Return to group and spend twenty minutes reflecting on the third "Dialogue with Jesus," found at www.upperroom.org/dialogues, and the questions there. In what ways do group members see Jesus offering good news and healing and confronting evil in this narrative from John's Gospel?

## CLOSURE (10 MINUTES)

Make any final preparations and announcements for your group retreat if necessary.

*Leader:* **In preparation for our next meeting** [in retreat or in your regular place of gathering], **read chapter 8, "Sustaining the Life and Ministry of God's Servants." Take time to respond prayerfully to the Reflection sections and to journal your responses. Bring your Bible, your book, and your journal to our next session.**

Close the group time in prayer.

Chapter 8

# Sustaining the Life and Ministry of God's Servants

*Blessed are the eyes that see what you see!*
*For I tell you that many prophets and kings desired to see*
*what you see, but did not see it, and to hear what you hear,*
*but did not hear it.—Luke 10:23-24*

While our gospel companions say little about their own experiences of outward ministry, they do draw our attention to several times when they regather. Simon Peter, Luke, and Matthew invite us to sit in alongside these early followers to hear what they share of their experience and then to hear Jesus' response. Enter prayerfully into their narrative in Mark 6:30-32; Luke 9:10; and Matthew 11:28-30.

## RHYTHM AND RULE OF LIFE AND MINISTRY

These early followers of Jesus draw our attention again to the rhythm of life and ministry that shapes and sustains their outward and inward journey: to come and be with Jesus; to receive guidance for personal and spiritual formation and service; to be sent out; and then to regather for rest and leisure, reporting in, praying, and receiving spiritual guidance.

This rhythm can become a model for our lives and ministry. Attention to rest and soul care can then inform the shape and content of our meetings with other servants of God. In this way the pastoral team, board members, teachers, youth ministers and sponsors, committee members, and those engaged in various forms of ministry within and beyond the church receive soul care and renewal.

When the disciples return from doing the work of ministry, Jesus invites them, "'Come away to a deserted place all by yourselves and rest a while.' For many were coming and going, and they had no leisure even to eat. And they went away in the boat to a deserted place by themselves" (Mark 6:31).

Today we rarely speak of leisure. But obviously Jesus included adequate time for rest and the invitation to stop, to do nothing. In our fast-paced world which measures success by what we achieve and what we can accumulate, our way of doing ministry can become driven by these narrow and oppressive measures. Hence we tend to resist the idea of pausing to withdraw for prayerful consideration of our acts of ministry and restful solitude for our own soul care. This is not just a present-day problem. In the twelfth century Bernard of Clairvaux wrote a letter to Eugenius, a former member of the monastic community of Clairvaux. Bernard continues as his spiritual director by reminding Eugenius to take time for prayerful reflection and meditation within the many demands of his new sphere of ministry as pope:

> If you wish to belong altogether to other people, like him who was made all things to all men, I praise your humanity, but only on condition that it be complete. But how can it be complete if you yourself are left out? You, too, are a man. So then, in order that your humanity may be entire and complete, let your bosom, which receives all, find room for yourself also. . . . In short if a man is bad to himself, to whom is he good? . . . [S]et aside some portion of your heart and of your time for consideration. . . . What is so essential to the worship of God as the practice to which He exhorts in the Psalm,

"Be still and know that I am God." This certainly is the chief object of consideration.[1]

## REFLECTION

How good to yourself are you? In what way are you arranging the flow of your schedule to include times of solitude, prayerful presence, reflection, and leisure?

---

## RETURN AND REGATHERING

On their return "the apostles gathered around Jesus" (Mark 6:30). The return is marked by coming—to be with Jesus and one another. This is a time for opening one's attention to Jesus and to the others present.

We can come to a meeting so full of our own agenda that we have little space for God or other persons present. As a result, we forget the intent for our return and regathering. Just as Jesus paid attention to the need of these disciples for solitude and rest, the person who convenes and who offers guidance for the gathering needs to pay attention to the hospitality of place and space in which the group is to meet. A place of meeting can offer its own invitation for rest and renewal.

### REPORTING IN

"[They] told him all they had done and taught" (Mark 6:30). Our gospel companions note that part of this regathering is given to telling Jesus all they had done and taught. Luke and Matthew offer us these conversations. Listen prayerfully as you read Luke 10:17-24.

Initially, reporting in is valuable because everyone gains an overview of ministry activity. With that larger picture in focus, we can then pause for prayerful reflection to discern where God is at work and toward what God invites our attention for ongoing ministry. The Holy Spirit may also assist us in noticing what may be missing in the picture.

A second value of reporting in emerges as we begin to notice where our ministry engagement evokes strong feelings. As we see in the account,

113

the disciples talk about acts of ministry that generate great excitement and joy. Jesus pays attention to their feelings and helps these gospel companions discern and own a deeper issue of their desire for power and domination.

A third value of checking in is the opportunity to note and own those times when our best efforts in ministry do not seem to work and we feel a sense of failure. The disciples also failed and came to Jesus with their disappointment and questions.

Finally, reporting in allows us to become aware of invitations to growth and discovery—both within ourselves and within our ministry.

## RECEIVING MINISTRY SUPERVISION AND SPIRITUAL GUIDANCE

We are invited first to sit alongside the disciples as they report in about acts of ministry that evoke feelings of joy and success when they respond to Jesus' call to confront evil:

> The seventy returned with joy, saying,
> "Lord, in your name even the demons submit to us!"
> (Luke 10:17)

As we listen to Jesus' response to the enthusiastic report of the seventy disciples, our gospel companions direct our attention to what Jesus sees and discerns and how he responds. First, he sets their particular work of ministry within the larger picture and context of kingdom and heavenly realities: "I watched Satan fall from heaven like a flash of lightning." Jesus reveals to us that Satan has lost his place of power within the heavenly realm, demonstrated by the demons' submission to the authority of Jesus.

What we do in response to God's call in pastoral ministry can sometimes seem small, insignificant, and earthbound. But ministry in the name of Jesus is a sign of the kingdom of God—the gracious rule of heaven showing up among us, here and now.

Jesus continues by directing the disciples' attention to the source of this authority to which the demons submit: "See, I have given you authority to tread on snakes and scorpions, and over all the power of the enemy, and nothing will hurt you."

This authority is a gift. The disciples—and we—are dependent on God, on Jesus, on the presence and work of the Holy Spirit in all that we do. Here we also catch the reassurance Jesus gives as he calls his disciples into this ministry of confronting spiritual powers. The demonic realm desires to evoke fear and render us powerless. Jesus assures us that we are empowered with his authority, and nothing can hurt us. Authority in the name of Jesus Christ gives us protection.

Jesus now turns the attention of these disciples to looking more closely at the source of their joy, an awareness absent from their report. "Nevertheless, do not rejoice at this, that the spirits submit to you, but rejoice that your names are written in heaven."

The disciples are reveling in the amount of power and authority they have received: Even the demons submit to them! Power can be seductive. Spiritual power can also entice. Jesus directs their attention to a deeper source of joy: not power over demons or demons' submission to them but rather their identity as children of God. They belong to the family of God, and their names are written in the birth records of heaven.

Identity, power, and authority rest in God. When we relinquish our need to prove who we are by using power and being in control, then we are able to discern the deceptive lure of our desire for domination.

Having domination over evil spirits can also produce an unhealthy preoccupation with evil, the demonic, and the realm of Satan. Enticement is one of Satan's strong weapons; think of how the serpent used it in the Garden. We can be lulled into a kind of stupor by evil and by our own desire. Both are designed to prevent our recognizing the attraction for what it is: something that lures us away from God and God's guidance.

Jesus faced his own experience of Satan's temptation to misuse power in the guise of accomplishing the work God had assigned him. Hence Jesus offers this spiritual guidance to our gospel companions and to us: "Do not rejoice at this, that the spirits submit to you, but rejoice that your names are written in heaven." Jesus is calling us to change our understanding of power. The source of our joy is discerned, challenged, and redirected.

## REFLECTION

- What excites you as you do the work of ministry?
- Where do you find your deepest joy?

———◦◦◦———

### PRAYER AND THANKFULNESS

Matthew and Luke remember Jesus offering prayer, thanksgiving, and blessing during their times of regathering. Listen prayerfully as you read Matthew 11:25-30 and Luke 10:21-24. Gather with the disciples alongside Jesus for a time of prayer.

> At that same hour Jesus rejoiced in the Holy Spirit and said, "I thank you, [Abba], Lord of heaven and earth, because you have hidden these things from the wise and the intelligent and have revealed them to infants; yes, [Abba], for such was your gracious will. All things have been handed over to me by my Father; and no one knows who the Son is except the Father, or who the Father is except the Son and anyone to whom the Son chooses to reveal him (Luke 10:21-22).

As Jesus prays we become aware of the Holy Spirit spilling over with joy and thankfulness within him. He is thankful that God is at work making him known. Jesus is also at work, making God known.

While we do the work of ministry, faithfully proclaiming, teaching, and healing, we are not able to make people see or understand the good news of the kingdom of God. This kind of knowing is a gift that God gives, God reveals, and that the Holy Spirit helps us see. God colabors with us through the presence of the Holy Spirit as we respond to Jesus' call to companion others into the kingdom.

Jesus turns to the disciples—and to us—and says:

> Blessed are the eyes that see what you see! For I tell you that many prophets and kings desired to see what you see, but did not see it, and to hear what you hear, but did not hear it (Luke 10:23-24).

You do see! Blessed are you! Here Jesus directs attention to the blessing we experience as we discern the inbreaking of the kingdom of God.

## Reflection

*Receiving rest for your soul.* In order for us to enter more fully into this reality and to know the rest that doing ministry within the kingdom perspective brings, Jesus concludes this time of retreat and spiritual guidance with a guided meditation. Matthew remembers these gentle words of Jesus. Hear Jesus speaking to you:

> Come to me, all you that are weary and are carrying heavy burdens, and I will give you rest. Take my yoke upon you, and learn from me; for I am gentle and humble in heart, and you will find rest for your souls. For my yoke is easy, and my burden is light (Matt. 11:28-30).

As you shift your attention away from your work and ministry responsibilities toward this quiet place with Jesus, listen to him calling you to come. What loads are you carrying? What weighs you down? What do you need to set down before Jesus?

Notice what is there. Pay attention to how Jesus responds to you and to what you have laid aside. Be in conversation with Jesus now. Listen to his guidance and help.

As you give up your load, Jesus offers you his yoke. The image suggests an experienced ox who knows the furrows of the field, who bears the weight of the work. The younger, inexperienced ox yoked alongside bears the light and easy end of the yoke. In this yoked companionship, the older ox leads, heaves, and carries the load, while the younger ox stays alongside, learning the ways of the field. Jesus goes the distance and knows the ways of the field of the harvest. We are called to stay close, in yoked companionship, and learn the ways of Jesus. In this way of being and doing we know rest, rest for our souls.

*Discernment.* In what ways were you surprised by the gentleness of Jesus' invitation to come and be with him?

- What was Jesus inviting you to bring and lay down?
- In what way are you noticing resistance, if any, to letting go of what you carry?
- How do you respond to receiving Jesus' yoke?

- How do you respond to receiving Jesus' guidance and help?
- In what ways are you aware of the rest Jesus gives?

―――――◦◉◦―――――

## WHEN ACTS OF MINISTRY SEEM TO FAIL

Our gospel companions ask us to be present with them as they describe an act of ministry that ended in disappointment and failure. Listen prayerfully as you enter the narrative in Mark 9:14-29 and Matthew 17:14-21.

Jesus and the disciples begin their regathering in the presence of the scribes, the crowd, and a distraught father who has brought his son to be healed. The scribes and the disciples are in a hot debate when Jesus arrives. In order for everyone to get a sense of what is going on, Jesus asks, "What are you arguing about with them?" Out of the crowd the voice of the troubled father sounds in reply:

> Teacher, I brought you my son; he has a spirit that makes him unable to speak; and whenever it seizes him, it dashes him down; and he foams and grinds his teeth and becomes rigid; and I asked your disciples to cast it out, but they could not do so (Mark 9:17-18).

In this instance, the father delivers the ministry report publicly, exposing before everyone the disciples' failure in their attempts to cure his son.

## RECEIVING MINISTRY SUPERVISION AND SPIRITUAL GUIDANCE

As his first act of ministry supervision, Jesus draws the disciples' attention—and ours—to the bigger picture, the larger sphere of unbelief in which they live and minister. "You faithless generation, how much longer must I be among you? How much longer must I put up with you?" Jesus laments (Mark 9:19).

As a Hebrew, Jesus draws us into the long tradition of lament—the prayer of complaint which gives permission to express sorrow, anger, fatigue, and any experience of painful disorientation.[2] Listening to Jesus' lament, our gospel companions recognize that they are more influenced than they realize by the lack of faith and the perverted belief systems of the larger society in which they live. Here we are given a lesson in contrast. Jesus lives, breathes, and acts from within the great reality of God's presence and gracious rule. He expresses his complaint in order to rescue their soul awareness, to free them from captivity to what is false, and to open their eyes to the freedom and healing of what is true. To help this lesson of spiritual guidance find lodging in their soul and experience, Jesus turns to the boy's father and the crowd and says: "Bring him to me."

The evil spirit within the boy now reacts to being in Jesus' presence, convulsing the boy, causing him to fall to the ground, to roll around, and to foam at the mouth. Demons do tend to act out, as if seeking to diminish our intent and weaken our faith in God's power to free us from their oppression. Rather than allow the demon's behavior to influence him, Jesus observes what is happening and seeks to discern the situation more fully. "How long has this been happening to him?" Jesus asks the father. The distraught father describes to Jesus how long his son has been so profoundly ill:

> From childhood. It has often cast him into the fire and into the water, to destroy him; but if you are able to do anything, have pity on us and help us (v. 22).

Jesus replies, "If you are able!—All things can be done for the one who believes." Again Jesus points to himself as the One who is able. The good news is that the gracious rule of God is here now among us! Jesus is caring for the father and for the child, even as he is giving guidance to the disciples.

Immediately the father of the child cries out, "I believe; help my unbelief!"

A shift is underway in how this father sees. He becomes aware of his own lack of trust, his own inability to believe that his son can be healed, and he brings this confession into his prayer and plea to Jesus.

In response, Jesus rebukes the unclean spirit, saying to it, "You spirit that keeps this boy from speaking and hearing, I command you, come out of him, and never enter him again!" (v. 25).

> After crying out and convulsing the boy terribly, it came out, and the boy was like a corpse, so that most of [the crowd] said, "He is

dead." But Jesus took him by the hand and lifted him up, and he was able to stand (vv. 26-28).

We are affected by the lack of faith and being present to God within the greater society in which we live. This pervasive disbelief eats away at our own faith and ability to be present, causing our trust to shrink into unbelief. We may not realize what has happened until we confront a situation where our ministry efforts result in failure. But failure is not final. God meets us in our failure and helps us discern a pathway to consolation and growth in faith.

Later, when the disciples come to Jesus for private conversation and reflection on this ministry event, they voice the question their failure evokes within them: "Why could we not cast it out?" (Matt. 17:19). Jesus responds with spiritual direction. He discerns two areas for attention and growth, the first of which is their lack of faith.

> Because of your little faith. For truly I tell you, if you have faith the size of a mustard seed, you will say to this mountain, "Move from here to there," and it will move; and nothing will be impossible for you (v. 20).

Situations we encounter in life and ministry can seem like mountains. Evil in this world and the power of the demonic realm are mountains that block our view of God's presence. Jesus, as spiritual director, is helping the disciples and us envision how to respond in the face of such enormous and threatening difficulty: Faith is turning to God.

The Holy Spirit assists us in this awareness about faith. We learn this turning to God, this waiting in simple trust, becoming aware of God's response to a situation as we pray. And prayer is the second area for which Jesus offers spiritual direction to our gospel companions: They need to learn to pray. "This kind can come out only through prayer" (Mark 9:29).

Faith grows as we learn to open our attention to God in prayer, to be present and available for God as we still ourselves, as we wait, and as we listen.

# Attending to Spiritual Guidance

## PREPARATION FOR REST AND PRAYER RETREAT

If possible, arrange with your ministry group to spend a day in retreat for this time of attending to spiritual guidance. In preparation for the retreat you will need persons to care for:

*The setting.* Pay attention to the place and space where the group will meet. Look for a private space free from interruptions, such as ringing phones. Consider how to arrange the chairs and create a worship center that invites prayerful attention. All these elements will evoke the intent and soul of the meeting.

*Hospitality.* Arrange to provide food, drinks, and other amenities.

*Worship sessions.* Plan for flow of the service, music, visual arts (A plant, a candle, or an object that symbolizes the retreat's theme can provide a focal point.).

*Guidance for overall schedule and retreat sessions.* Attend to schedule by incorporating a rhythm of gathering and solitude—gathering to learn, time in solitude for reflection, time for one-on-one conversation, group sharing, worship.

*Handouts.* Make copies of the session outlines and meditation guides given in this chapter.

## SUGGESTED SCHEDULE FOR RETREAT

### ARRIVAL AND SETTLING IN (30 MINUTES)

### WORSHIP (30 MINUTES)

- Gathering, being present to one another.
- *Leader:* **Our gospel companions invite us to retreat, to be in a quiet place for rest and prayerful solitude.**

- Singing
- Opening prayer
- Opening our attention to one another: Invite each person to share what he or she desires in this time of retreat.
- Opening our attention to God.

*Leader:* Hear the invitation of Jesus in Matthew 11:28-30: "Come to me, all of you that are weary and are carrying heavy burdens, and I will give you rest." (Silence) Jesus is here, inviting us to come. Inviting you to come. (Silence)

Notice your tiredness. Pay attention to the loads you carry. Bring your tiredness and the loads you carry to Jesus. Lay them down. Jesus says: "Here you will find rest for your souls. I will give you rest." (Silence)

- Singing
- Prayer. Invite the help and companioning of the Holy Spirit.

## FIRST SESSION (1 ½ HOURS)

## ENTERING INTO RETREAT

### READING (15 MINUTES)

Read Luke 11:1-13. Invite participants to enter the narrative. Read Luke 11:1-4 again.

*Leader:* The spiritual guidance Jesus gave to the disciples during their time together in ministry supervision sinks like a seed into the soil of their souls. In this quiet, fertile place the invitation to learn to pray begins to root itself in their consciousness. Some time later, as they are in retreat and Jesus withdraws to pray, the seed bears fruit. Our gospel companions begin to voice their desire for help in learning to pray: "Lord, teach us to pray, as John taught his disciples." Jesus offers spiritual guidance about how to pray.

> When you pray, say
> [Abba], hallowed by your name.
> Your kingdom come.
> Your will be done,
>   on earth as it is in heaven.
> Give us this day our daily bread,

And forgive us our debts,
  as we also have forgiven our debtors.
And do not bring us into the time of trial,
  but rescue us from the evil one.

No matter where Christian believers gather or from which background or language we come, we all know this prayer, and we all pray it. Sometimes we say the words but do not pray as we speak.

Pray the Lord's Prayer together.

## MEDITATION (1 HOUR)

In this time of retreat you are invited to pray this prayer slowly, one line at a time. Meditate on the words, the phrases; allow the prayer to sink deep into your soul and being. Pay attention to what Jesus offers in the way of focus, intent, and content. You have one hour for this time of prayer and reflection.

## SHARING (15 MINUTES)

Meet in pairs to share some of your discoveries.

## BREAK AND REST (1 HOUR)

Provide something to drink and a snack or a lunch.

## SECOND SESSION (2 HOURS)

# THE DILEMMA OF MINISTRY

## RECOGNIZING THE LIMITS OF OUR STRENGTH AND LEARNING TO WAIT ON GOD'S GUIDANCE

## READING (40 MINUTES)

Read Luke 11:5-13 aloud twice.

*Leader:* Jesus draws our attention first to a dilemma in verses 5–7. Ministry in the name of Jesus is a sacred trust. The call of God on our lives is to bring good news, to offer:

- good news of life rather than death,
- community rather than oppressive loneliness,

- sight rather than blindness,
- freedom from slavery to all that controls and holds us captive.

With this sacred nature of ministry in mind, Jesus draws the attention of our gospel companions into the dilemma of being unable to rely on their own strength for pursuing ministry.

The Hebrews understood hospitality to friends and strangers as a sacred duty. This hospitable and holy act of providing welcome, shelter, and sustenance followed the example of Abraham and Sarah who offered rest, foot washing, and food to the three strangers in Genesis 18. Within the presence of the stranger is God: In welcoming and making space for others, people welcome God.[3]

Jesus presents a scenario that puts the gospel companions in the place of a host caught with no food in the house, at a bad time—midnight—when all the stores are closed, and when neighbors are asleep for the night. A host caught in a sacred dilemma: needing to provide but having nothing to offer. However, the host decides to turn to a friend. At first the friend does not want to be bothered: His door is locked, his children are asleep, he cannot get up, and he cannot provide anything.

Take a few minutes to reflect on your own experience of being caught in such a dilemma: not having what is needed for the sacred tasks of ministry. You are empty-handed. When you ask for help, at first nothing seems to happen.

Read Luke 11:5-10.

*Leader:* Now Jesus turns the attention of his disciples toward the need to keep on seeking. He tells them to be persistent, to keep asking, and to keep knocking. Such persistence is rewarded. What they need for the sacred tasks of hospitable ministry will be provided!

Prayer is not learned in an hour nor in a day. Prayer is learned

- as we ask and then listen—and notice what is given;
- as we search—and notice what is revealed to us;
- as we knock—and notice what begins to open up.

In our fast-paced culture we may become impatient because the answers we seek do not show up immediately. We may judge God to be disinterested, in bed with his door locked and unwilling to get up to provide. But Jesus challenges our images and concepts of God by turning our attention to how we respond to our own children, we who are imperfect and human parents. We do know how to give what is good to our children.

Take time now to be in the presence of God with your needs. Simply bring them to God and then wait. Notice anything you hear, anything that is given you in the way of guidance, and anything that seems to open up for you. Possibly nothing will happen, but the invitation is still to wait, to simply be in God's presence.

Allow five minutes of silent, prayerful reflection before continuing. Read Luke 11:5-13 again.

*Leader:* Finally, Jesus invites us to turn our attention away from what we consider our immediate and pressing needs in ministry and to open our gaze to the hospitality of our heavenly Abba. God gives the Holy Spirit. The Holy Spirit comes alongside us to help, companion, and dwell in us to reveal the presence of Jesus, of God. Listen to what Jesus has to say.

Meditate on the following passage in the form of *lectio divina*. First we'll read the text aloud twice together: During the second reading stop when a word or phrase "shimmers" or stands out for you. This may not be a strong awareness, but when a word or a phrase slows your attention, stop reading. The gradual shift as each person stops reading aloud and moves into silent meditation signals the presence and prompting of the Holy Spirit. Meditate on the word or phrase. Allow it to sound slowly within you; repeat the phrase and let its meaning to sink gradually deeper into your awareness. Be hospitable to the word entering into all the rooms of your life.

> I will ask the Father, and he will give you another Advocate, to be with you forever. This is the Spirit of truth, whom the world cannot receive, because it neither sees him nor knows him. You know him, because he abides with you, and he will be in you. I will not leave you orphaned; I am coming to you. . . . On that day you will know that I am in my Father, and you in me, and I in you . . . .

Those who love me will keep my word, and my Father will love them and we will come to them, and make our home with them. . . . I am the vine, you are the branches. Those who abide in me and I in them bear much fruit, because apart from me you can do nothing "(John 14:16-18, 20, 23; 15:5).

**Respond to God in prayer about what you are discovering as God uses the word to read your life. Then be still and simply rest in the spacious and gracious presence of God.**

## REFLECTION (1 HOUR)

Allow one hour for solitude and prayerful reflection. The following questions may be used as guidelines.

- How has God's presence and care surprised you through praying the scripture?
- What dilemma did you bring to God, and how did you feel about that problem or need?
- What has God shown you, opened up to you?
- In what way were you aware of the help and guidance of the Holy Spirit assisting you as you meditated?
- For what are you thankful?

## SHARING (20 MINUTES)

Regather. Have beverages available. Share your discoveries one-on-one.

## BREAK (15 MINUTES)

This time offers the gift of not needing to do anything. Nothing is required or asked of participants.

## REGATHERING AND CLOSING WORSHIP (1 HOUR)

Share discoveries together as a group. Conclude with worship the group has prepared. Include a few minutes to remind group members to read chapter 9 in preparation for the next session together.

*Leader:* **As before, pay prayerful attention to the Reflection sections included in the text and journal your responses. Bring a copy of the book, your Bible, and journal with you for use in the session.**

# Tending the Field of the Heart

*Blessed [are those] who[se] . . . delight is in the law of*
*the LORD, and on his law [they] meditate day and night.*
—Psalm 1:1, NIV

In explaining the parable of the sower and the seed, Jesus lays out a map for the inward journey. As spiritual director he gives patient attention to the heart condition of the disciples and others with whom he engages. The work of God within the heart takes time. At first the early disciples do not comprehend what Jesus is doing or saying. But in time, as he continues this patient field work, they realize their need for deep, inner transformation. They direct our attention to the seasons of life when we are more receptive to this divine plowing:

> when expectations are challenged;
> when we confront the impossible;
> when obedience is difficult and costly;
> when obedience is criticized.

Pause and be prayerfully present as you enter Simon Peter's narrative in Mark 6:33-44. John and Matthew also come alongside with their memory of the event: John 6:1-14; Matthew 14:13-21. Ask the Holy Spirit to help you notice how God may be at work in your own heart field.

## WHEN EXPECTATIONS ARE CHALLENGED

The disciples respond to Jesus' invitation to be in retreat as they leave Capernaum and sail across the lake, but when they moor their boat, a great crowd is forming on the shore. To our surprise Jesus does not ask the disciples to put out to sea again; nor does he dismiss the crowd. Instead, he looks out over these thousands of people and sees them as sheep without a shepherd, lost and directionless, unable to find their way home to the gracious presence and rule of God. Moved with compassion, Jesus changes his plans. The expectation for rest and retreat is placed on hold.

I was on my way home from the seminary following a heavy day of pastoral care and looked forward to being home. I had gone about a half mile after turning off the main highway when I saw cows in the road ahead; I slowed the car and came to a stop. About thirty Holstein cattle had broken through some fencing and were intent on following each other out of the field. Loud bellowing announced their anxiety as they crowded into the road and the ditch on the far side. It did not occur to them to turn back and reenter the pasture. So there the cows stood—anxious, noisy, bewildered.

I wondered what I should do since I was unfamiliar with the ways of cattle, and I was not sure of the farm owner's name. How long would it be before these cows got out of the way so that I could go on my way home? This last thought, I confess, was uppermost in my mind. Just then I saw a man walking down the lane beside the field. He had heard the bellowing and was coming to see what the ado was about. Calmly, quietly, he walked into the midst of the herd, made his way across the road, and stood on one side of the ditch. Then he began waving his arms. Just as I was wondering what his waving was about and what it could accomplish in such a situation, I realized that this is what the cows needed. One by one they quieted their loud lament and turned back toward the direction from which they had come. The farmer continued to wave his arms until all thirty had ambled slowly back across the road and into the field. Then he crossed the road, gave me a smile and a wave, and began putting the fence to rights.

We forget that God is the owner of the farm, the shepherd who notices when we are lost. And so we tend to see the crowd as an intrusion, getting in the way of our plans and agenda. But Jesus sees the people as sheep without a shepherd, crowding at the edge of the lake and needing direction to find their way home to the kingdom of God's gracious rule. Many years before, the prophet Ezekiel had heard God say:

> I myself will search for my sheep, and will seek them out. As shepherds seek out their flocks when they are among their scattered sheep, so I will seek out my sheep. I will rescue them from all the places to which they have been scattered . . . I will feed them with good pasture . . . I myself will be the shepherd of my sheep, and I will make them lie down, says the Lord God. I will seek the lost, and I will bring back the strayed, and I will bind up the injured, and I will strengthen the weak (Ezek. 34:11-12, 14-16).

Jesus is that shepherd, and so he responds by healing the sick and then teaching the crowd (Mark 6:34). We may respond to this passage in Mark by thinking that times of retreat are not needed, no matter how stressed and busy our ministry. After all, Jesus continued to serve the crowd and called the disciples to do the same. We are in danger of being caught in the ministerial temptation of needing to rescue everyone—trying to be savior—if we find ourselves continually postponing times for solitude, prayer, and rest in favor of people's needs. Throughout the gospel narrative, the disciples take us with them on numerous retreats. Jesus practiced a steady rhythm of ministry engagement and prayerful withdrawal. The invitation here is to be flexible and open to the flow of God's compassion and guidance rather than fixated on our expectations.

Our gospel companions admit that they were slow to learn this lesson of availability to God's initiative. By late afternoon they feel tired and inhospitable to the needs of the crowd. They interrupt Jesus' teaching and remind him, "This is a deserted place. The hour is now very late;

send them away so that they may go into the surrounding country and villages and buy something for themselves to eat."

They are not ready for his reply: "They need not go away; you give them something to eat."

## WHEN WE CONFRONT THE IMPOSSIBLE

From the standpoint of these disciples, things had moved from bad to worse and have now sunk to the impossible. Jesus has told them to do an act of ministry for which they have little or no resources. John remembers Jesus turning to Philip and asking, "Where are we to buy bread for these people to eat?" Philip remembers standing there, scanning the crowd. His first thought was to calculate the cost of feeding five thousand people. However, after a quick count he replies, "Six months' wages of a day laborer wouldn't buy enough bread for each person to even have a little." He could think only of the money needed, and he knew they didn't have enough in their common purse to even think of buying bread.

John allows us entry now into the mind and intention of Jesus: Jesus already knew what he was going to do. He questioned Philip in order to help this disciple get in touch with himself on a deeper level. Providing bread in this deserted place was not a problem for Jesus. Abba God had done this every day for his people when the Hebrews journeyed for forty years through the vast stretches of wilderness between Egypt and Canaan. However, Jesus was doing more than providing bread for the multitude. He was helping Philip and the disciples learn to move beyond trusting in a response grounded solely in human logic.

Neither Philip nor the other gospel companions know what is going on. In a later conversation, Jesus tells them the problem is their hardened hearts. They are resistant to learning God's way of doings things. That resistance explains why Philip turns first to doing the statistics and concludes that feeding the crowd is an impossibility. He is living and acting in the sphere of his human and rational ego self. This sphere may be of assistance as far as facts and statistics go, but it is not the only place to turn in response to God's invitations in ministry.

Quaker writer and spiritual director Thomas Kelly says, "There is a way of ordering our mental life on more than one level at once. On one level we may be thinking, discussing, seeing, calculating, meeting all the demands of external affairs. But deep within, behind the scenes, at a profounder level, we may also be in prayer . . . and a gentle receptiveness to divine breathings."[1] Kelly goes on to say that people in today's world value and cultivate the first level of thinking, while the deeper level tends to be questioned, mildly tolerated, or even scorned.[2] Such is the division we live in, as we discovered in chapter 2. However, if we can offer the gifts of this "upper level" to God, they can be servants of the gospel rather than hostile committee members around our mental table, each vying for power and supremacy, ignoring God's presence and divine breathings.

In the face of the impossible, we are invited to acknowledge our emptiness and poverty and wait for God's response. Listening for divine breathings is not something we do easily. We recognize the "honkings" of God only over time. And just as our gospel companions needed the spiritual direction Jesus offered, so we also will need the help of a wise and discerning spiritual guide when facing impasse and the impossible.

## WHEN OBEDIENCE IS DIFFICULT AND COSTLY

The multitude is aware of the miracle they have just witnessed—and eaten! They begin to move toward Jesus, wanting to force him to become king. But Jesus knows the reasons for their surge of desire. In their excitement over the healings, the miraculous provision of food, and Jesus' teaching, the crowd hopes to force Jesus' hand and start a revolution against the Roman government by making him king. Jesus already has faced into the temptation to win the world by adopting its ways; instead of being drawn into the demands of the crowd, he tells his followers to start back across the lake while he dismisses the people. Join the disciples on this long and difficult night crossing as you enter the narrative in Mark 6:33-44 (see also John 6:1-14 and Matt. 14:13-21). Jesus goes up on the mountain to pray. As evening falls, he is in retreat with Abba.

It has been a long, tiring day, and, adding to the disciples' weariness, a strong wind troubles the waters. Seasoned fishermen, they strain at the oars through the night hours, making little progress against the stormy sea. As dawn breaks, they have rowed only about three or four miles and are bone weary. Their fatigue lurches into terror when they see a figure walking on the water in the half-light of dawn. Is it a ghost? Terrified, the disciples cry out. In return, the strange presence speaks comfort; the voice is familiar: "Take heart, it is I; do not be afraid" (Mark 6:50).

Long night vigils with their weight of fatigue can result in spiritual night blindness. We no longer recognize God's ways of coming to us. And we may make rash decisions. Matthew remembers Simon's reaction: "Lord, if it is you, command me to come to you on the water." "Come," Jesus says (Matt. 14:28, 29). We watch as Peter gets out of the boat and begins walking toward Jesus. A few steps into this watery path Peter becomes aware of the strength of the wind, and suddenly fear kidnaps his attention. He begins to sink into the sea. Although he is an experienced fisherman, in his fatigue and terror he forgets he can swim and cries out to Jesus, "Lord, save me!" Jesus responds immediately and reaches out his hand to catch him. As he pulls Peter up out of the churning waters, Jesus says, "You of little faith, why did you doubt?" (Matt 14:30, 31).

The question is not just for Simon to ponder. Jesus asks it of all of us. Why do we doubt? What keeps our faith so small? And how do we get kidnapped out of believing, trusting? Just what are we afraid of?

Jesus and Peter climb into the boat, and the wind finally stops. It is as if the wind lies down in the presence of its Creator and Lord. The waters also become calm. The disciples row the boat to shore, climb out onto dry land—weary, confused, their bodies aching and their souls full of fearful wonder.

## REFLECTION

Look back over your own experience of ministry. Pay attention to those seasons in your life when God was at work, plowing the soil of your soul: when expectations were challenged, when situations were impossible, when obedience was difficult and costly.

- What was your immediate response?
- How did you pray? How do you listen for divine breathings?
- In what way are you aware of God's help and guidance?
- How are you aware of God's tending the field of your soul?

---

## WHEN OBEDIENCE IS CRITICIZED

Read Mark 7:1-23; 8:1-26; Matthew 23:1-35.

Teresa of Avila writes, "We have heard and because faith tells us so, we know we have souls. But we seldom consider the precious things that can be found in this soul, or who dwells within it." In her work as spiritual director, Teresa calls us to enter into our souls, to be present to ourselves and to God who dwells within us. We enter into our heart through the doors of prayer and reflection.[3] Not to enter is to keep our distance. Jesus now speaks to this avoidance and distancing. Simon Peter invites us into the narrative in Mark 6:53–7:23; 8:11-21. Matthew also remembers in Matthew 23:1-35.

The conversation begins as our guides on this gospel pilgrimage lead us into villages near the north end of the lake. The disciples call us to watch Jesus respond to the scores of people who come, some laying their sick in the marketplaces, asking if they might touch even the fringe of his clothes. In his kindness and compassion, Jesus offers healing to all.

The Pharisees and the scribes are also watching. However, their attention is fixed on guarding the religious rituals and traditions that Jesus' followers do not observe. These religious leaders gather around Jesus and ask, "Why do your disciples not live according to the tradition of the elders, but eat with defiled hands?" (7:5). In response Jesus chooses to address what lies at the root of their question and their practice:

> Isaiah prophesied rightly about you hypocrites, as it is written,
> "This people honors me with their lips,
>  but their hearts are far from me;
> in vain do they worship me,
>  teaching human precepts as doctrines."

You abandon the commandment of God and hold to human
tradition (vv. 6-8).

Here Jesus clearly and incisively lays open the condition of their
lives. Worship has become meaningless word-service because the heart
stands apart from God, distant. Hardness of heart reveals itself in lack
of spiritual insight, in attitudes and behaviors that diminish and deny
others while serving the self. These religious people have tied religious
observance to rules that govern the keeping of the law, negating the spirit
and intent of God's way. This human tradition becomes a heavy burden
laid upon the shoulders of the people, who are required to pay meticu-
lous attention to outward matters but ignore the hungers and condition
of their hearts. Matthew remembers Jesus' impassioned confrontation of
the scribes and Pharisees about their need to look within:

> Woe to you, scribes and Pharisees, hypocrites! For you clean the out-
> side of the cup and of the plate, but inside [you] are full of greed
> and self-indulgence. You blind Pharisee! First clean the inside of the
> cup, so that the outside also may become clean (Matt. 23:25-26).

Hence Jesus warns his followers: "Watch out—beware of the yeast
of the Pharisees," that is, their hypocrisy (Mark 8:15). Their narrow way
of seeing prevents them from recognizing the Great Sign of God in the
person of Jesus standing in their presence and in the miracles of healing
and reconciliation he offers. Instead, the Pharisees come and argue with
him, demanding that he produce a sign from heaven. Our gospel companions remember Jesus responding with a deep sigh, a sigh that emerges
from the depths of his spirit. He asks, "Why does this generation ask for
a sign?" (Mark 8:11-12).

We tend to look for outward signs: Do those people dress as we do?
What is the style of their worship? Do they worship as we do? What religious label do they wear: evangelical? conservative? social activist? charis-
matic? liberal? orthodox? While describing our way of living and worship
can be helpful in our understanding of one another, labels can also result
in distancing and denial. The Pharisees labeled those who did not believe
and practice as they did unclean, defiled.

Simon Peter absorbs Jesus' teaching and learns how to cope with criticism. Out of his own heart experience he gives spiritual guidance to believers in the church.

> "If you . . . suffer for doing what is right, you are blessed. Do not fear what they fear, and do not be intimidated, but in your hearts sanctify Christ as Lord" (1 Pet. 3:14-15).

Simon invites us to notice what is within the heart and to see the Lord Jesus Christ also present. He calls on us to see Jesus creating a sacred space within our heart and being. As we move toward Jesus, we are freed from the fear and intimidation caused by destructive criticism.

## REFLECTION

Envision your own heart space—the field of your soul. Jesus is there, waiting for you to come and be with him. Once you have a sense of Jesus' presence, recall a time when you were criticized or judged as you followed Jesus in ministry. Get in touch with your feelings. Ask Jesus to help you see the event—what was said or done—as he sees.

*Discernment*
- What do you notice?
- What is Jesus' invitation to you? How do you respond?

## SEEING WITHIN: UNCOVERING THE HEART

Our gospel companions soon realize that not only religious leaders have heart trouble. They themselves suffer from hardness of heart and lack of spiritual perception, both part of our human condition. So Jesus calls the crowd to hear a short parable along with the disciples: "Listen to me, all of you, and understand: there is nothing outside a person that by going in can defile, but the things that come out are what defile" (Mark 7:14-15).

In response to the disciples' request for clarification, Jesus explains that we are defiled by what comes from within us, from the human heart. This is the place from which evil intentions come. Now he gives a list of what indwells us, naming the faces of evil and its intent: fornication, theft, murder, adultery, avarice, wickedness, deceit, licentiousness, envy, slander, pride, folly. All these evil intentions come from within, and they defile a person. Evagrius Ponticus, one of the desert fathers of the early fourth century, counseled others by saying, "It is not in our power to determine whether we are disturbed by these thoughts, but it is up to us to decide if they are to linger within us or not and whether or not they are to stir up our passions."[4]

James, the Lord's brother, later in life recognizes the movement and intent of evil within the heart. He shares the insights he has received in a letter to other believers:

> One is tempted by one's own desire, being lured and enticed by it; then, when that desire has conceived, it gives birth to sin, and that sin, when it is fully grown, gives birth to death. Do not be deceived, my beloved (Jas. 1:14-15).

Rather than live in denial, we are invited by Jesus to reckon honestly and openly with what is within our being. Jeremiah notes that our heart is devious, perverse. He wonders who can understand it. In response to this question, God replies, "I the LORD test [discern and know] the mind and search the heart" (Jer. 17:10).

## REFLECTION

Envision God coming to the gate of your heart field. Jesus is the divine plowman and asks you to open the gate. You may sense that certain rocks of doubt and fear lie in the field. Evil intentions may also infest part of the field. Hear Jesus saying to you, "Do not be afraid." As you open the gate, you are invited to pray,

> Search me, O God, and know my heart;
>     [discern] and know my thoughts.
> See if there is any harmful way in me,
>     and lead me in the way everlasting
> (Ps. 139:23-24).

*Discernment*

- In what ways are you more aware of the inward journey?
- In what ways are you receptive to God's tending the soil of your heart?
- How are you confessing your resistance?

# Attending to Spiritual Guidance

## GATHERING AND SETTLING IN (15 MINUTES)

*Leader:* Last time we met, we were on retreat, learning to pray, to trust in God's help, and to welcome the indwelling and work of the Holy Spirit. Today we are reflecting on chapter 9, paying attention to how God tends the field of our souls. For our opening meditation, we are invited to think about the people among whom we minister and the seasons in their lives when God plows and tends the field of their lives. We will spend twenty minutes in the meditation and ten minutes sharing one-on-one our response to the discernment questions.

Let us pray together and open our own heart to God.

*Prayer:* Loving and listening God, you see our inner heart. You come to indwell us, making your home within us. Help us by your Spirit to make our home with you. In the name of Jesus, Amen.

## MEDITATION (30 MINUTES)

In the congregation (or other places of ministry) where you serve, persons are experiencing seasons in their lives when God desires to plow and tend the field of their hearts. Envision the persons among whom you minister and the seasons of their lives and pause in silence as you think of them:

- Persons whose expectations are challenged (pause for one minute);
- Persons who are confronted with the impossible (pause);
- Those who are finding obedience to God difficult and costly (pause);
- Those who are criticized for their obedience (pause).

Notice where Jesus is for these persons in the seasons they are experiencing. Watch as Jesus works and tends the soil of their hearts.

**Thank God for the work God is doing in the lives of the congregation.**

*Discernment*
- **What did you notice?**
- **How did you respond?**
- **In what way is Jesus inviting you to colabor with him in this patient and loving work of tending the field of the soul?**

Share responses to the discernment questions one-on-one, taking five minutes each.

## GROUP REFLECTION (1 HOUR)

Invite group members to choose one of the seasons described in this chapter. Take turns sharing your experience with the group.

- What was the season?
- What did you experience?
- In what ways were you aware of God's presence, tending the soil of your heart in this season?
- How did you respond to God's knowing your heart and plowing the soil there?

**Listen carefully with grace and hospitality. You are privileged to be given insight into the sacred ground within one another's souls.**

## CLOSURE (15 MINUTES)

**Our assignment this week is to read chapter 10 and to journal our responses to the Reflection sections. Also take time to reflect on your experience of being a listener, using questions at the end of chapter 9. Write your responses in your journal.**

**We will close by praying for one another, inviting God's protection and companioning as the Spirit of Jesus tends the soil of our own hearts and the hearts of those among whom we serve.**

## ASSIGNMENT

Reflect on your experience of listening and journal responses to the following questions:

- In what ways am I being attentive and hospitable as I listen?
- What seems to kidnap my attention?
- What helps me to return to being open and receptive?
- In which ways am I becoming aware of areas for growth?
- How is this attending to spiritual guidance one-on-one and in group helping me listen to persons in the congregation and parish in which I worship and serve?

Chapter 10

# Discerning Revelation, Resisting Suffering

*Blessed are you. . . . For flesh and blood has not revealed*
*this to you, but my Father in heaven.—Matthew 16:17*

Jesus leaves Capernaum now to head north into the area of Caesarea Philippi and the Mount Hermon mountains. Here the River Jordan finds its source among mountain springs and streams. Our gospel companions invite us to join them in a quiet place near the villages of Caesarea Philippi. This is a time of being with, of naming and knowing—a time for retreat before Jesus begins the long walk toward Jerusalem and all that awaits him there. Read Luke 9:18-22; Mark 8:27–9:1; and Matthew 16:13-23 prayerfully as you enter the narrative.

Jesus prays. The disciples wait. Passover, the high festival of liberation of their people, is close. Will this be the time for Jesus to declare himself the son of David, Messiah, and for him to take over the throne and be ruler of Israel? Jesus interrupts their musings with another question: "Who do people say that I am?" (Mark 8:27). Our gospel companions reflect back on what they have heard people say during their travels in ministry throughout Galilee, Samaria, and Judea. "Some say John the Baptist," they reply, "but others Elijah, and still others Jeremiah or one of the prophets" (Matt. 16:14). Obviously people do not see Jesus as any ordinary man.

Now Jesus asks another, more personal question: "But who do you say that I am?" Simon Peter speaks what they are sensing in their hearts but are slow to find words for: "You are the Messiah, the Son of the living God." Jesus' response to Simon's confession is warm and affirming: "Blessed are you, Simon son of Jonah! For flesh and blood has not revealed this to you, but my Father in heaven" (Matt. 16:15-17).

We, along with Simon, are being invited by Jesus to learn about *how* we know. We can receive knowledge from rational, empirical human sources, but another source of knowing exists—revelation. Jesus reveals the heart of the new thing God is doing: No longer will a person's standing with God be built on keeping the law of Moses. Jesus is building the church—the household of God—on the sure foundation of believing he is the Messiah. We are transformed as we live into being children of God and sisters and brothers to one another. This is the great homecoming for which we all long.

## RESISTANCE TO SUFFERING

If the disciples are basking in the warmth of receiving spiritual insight into God's revelation about Jesus, quite suddenly their comfort level is shattered. Jesus informs them "he must go to Jerusalem and undergo great suffering at the hands of the elders and chief priest and scribes, and be killed, and on the third day be raised" (Matt. 16:21). The words sound dark, impossible, unreal. Our gospel companions share with us their reactions of shock, denial, and disbelief. Their understanding of the Messiah does not include suffering and death.

In his insightful work about Jewish life, personhood, and faith, Chaim Potok, Jewish rabbi and writer, illustrates something of the disciples' understanding in a mother's response to her artistic son, Asher Lev. Asher Lev questions her about paintings he has seen in an art museum in New York, paintings of Jesus being crucified.

"Why did the Romans kill Jesus?"

"He said he was the moshiach. They thought he would make a revolution against them."

"Was he the moshiach, Mama?"

"No. He was not the moshiach. The moshiach has not yet come, Asher. Look how much suffering there is in the world. Would there be so much suffering if the moshiach had really come?"[1]

Each time Jesus reveals what will happen to him—and to them—in Jerusalem, our gospel companions react by denying suffering. In their narratives these companions on pilgrimage confess the various ways they find to insulate themselves from the painful threat of losing their messianic dreams.

## SIMON PETER: DENIAL AND REBUKE

Peter walks Jesus away from the disciples a short distance and gives him a sharp rebuke: "God forbid it, Lord! This must never happen to you!" (Matt. 16:22). He calls on God to act in accordance with his own conception of the Messiah. Jesus turns his back on Peter and looks toward the rest of our disciple companions, his body language announcing the verbal rebuke he is about to give Peter: "Get behind me, Satan! You are a stumbling block to me; for you are setting your mind not on divine things but on human things" (v. 23).

Satan has not given up. Earlier in Jesus' life, Satan took Jesus to a high mountain and showed him all the kingdoms of the world and their splendor, offering them to Jesus if he would fall down and worship him (Luke 4:5-7). Now Satan is slipping through the cracks in Simon's limited belief system, trying to entrap Jesus in the lure of adopting world-power tactics as Messiah and avoiding the cross. Hence Jesus' sharp response. The same Simon Peter whom Jesus affirmed and blessed for embracing what God had revealed to him now receives rebuke for embracing what has been instigated by the devil.

The spiritual realm is not all benign. Jesus calls his disciples to discern what kind of spirit is at work within them as he explains to Peter,

"You are setting your mind not on divine things but on human things."

"Divine things" would include suffering, rejection, the cross, and the amazing triumph of the resurrection. It is to God's way of bringing us home that Jesus gives his time and attention. This is where he sets his mind. By remembering this spiritual direction Jesus offered Simon Peter, our gospel companions acknowledge that this guidance is directed to them and to us as we listen to Jesus' words. Later Peter could offer this same guidance to believers: "Prepare your minds for action; discipline yourselves; set all your hope on the grace that Jesus Christ will bring you when he is revealed. Like obedient children, do not be conformed to the desires that you formerly had in ignorance" (1 Pet. 1:13-14).

The desert fathers and mothers paid attention to this discipline of setting their minds on God and described the struggle they encountered. Abba Serenus knew the movement and countermovement well. "When we think that our heart is stretching out toward its goal, our mind, insensibly turned away from that to its former wanderings by a powerful impetus, slips away and, preoccupied with commonplace distractions, is so frequently captivated by so many things that we almost despair of the correction that we long for."[2] Rather than give up in despair, this spiritual director discerns that "it is in our power to set up in our hearts either ascents, which are thoughts that touch God, or descents, which sink down to earthly and carnal things."[3] It is not that our thoughts do not "sink down"; they do, but we are invited to turn once again toward God, toward God's loving and gracious ways in us and among us.

The idea of setting our mind on God's ways may sound like fixating our attention on some heavenly plane, far removed from the painful realities of this world. We need only to hear the words of Jesus to dispel any such notion.

> If any want to become my followers, let them deny themselves and take up their cross and follow me. For those who want to save their life will lose it (Matt. 16:24).

Whatever we worry about, strain after, become protective or violent about, and spend our life trying to save will, in the end, blind us to our real life—our soul and being. We will lose the very thing for which we have been concerned along with our true life and being; hence our need to pay attention to our hopes and desires. These things we offer to God; they become our sacrifice. Jesus continues:

> Those who lose their life for my sake will find it. For what will it profit them if they gain the whole world and forfeit their life? Or what will they give in return for their life (Matt. 16:25-26)?

## REFLECTION

- Jesus asks you: "Who do you say that I am?" Who is Jesus for you?
- How does God care for your material needs?
- How does God care for you in suffering? in rejection?
- To what are you being asked to die in order to follow Jesus in all of life?

---

## SIMON PETER: MAKING PLANS

Jesus walks farther north into the higher mountain elevations, taking Peter, James, and John with him. Listen as Simon Peter invites us to be present at this mountain retreat. Read Mark 9:2-10; Luke 9:28-36.

Jesus is praying. As sometimes happens when we pray, the disciples get tired. Tiredness may result from fatigue, boredom, stress, or resistance to being with God. At other times, when God desires to reveal something, God's presence and activity can awaken our soul, mind, and body. The disciples are suddenly pulled out of sleep by such a revelation: the dazzling appearance of Jesus and the presence of Moses and Elijah, who talk with him about his departure from Jerusalem. Not only are they jerked awake, but they are terrified.

When terror kidnaps us, we react in many different ways. Peter began by making plans to build shelters for the heavenly guests. Later he admits he did not know what he was saying. Planning for action manifested his way of dealing with fear. Being busy can build a wall around us and within us, keeping fear at bay, and preventing persons from coming close. Action also can create a wall between us and God, keeping God at a distance.

God responds by surrounding these fearful disciples with a cloud. At first the cloud feels just as frightening, but then a voice breaks through their fear and terror into their souls: "This is my Son, the Beloved; with him I am well pleased." God brings direction—pointing to Jesus the Beloved Son—and God gives direction: "Listen to him!" (Matt. 17:5). This cloud experience signals these men to unlearn what they think they know regarding the Messiah and to learn who Jesus truly is.

Such unlearning is a profound act of letting go of our prejudgments and preconceived ideas. A fourteenth-century anonymous spiritual director wrote at length describing this experience of not knowing and says "it is usual to feel nothing but a darkness about your mind, or as it were a cloud of unknowing. . . . Learn to be at home in this darkness."[4] We need to let go of our prejudgments in order to receive the knowings God gives us.

## REFLECTION

Enter into the gospel narrative on the mountain and be present as God speaks to you in the cloud. Be silent; listen. Contemplate what God says; then be present and quiet. Allow yourself simply to be in God's presence. If your mind wanders, return to being present by repeating God's words to you: "This is my Son, the Beloved. Listen to him!" Resist the temptation to make plans or be busy—as Simon Peter tried to do. Simply be present. Take twenty minutes for this contemplative prayer exercise.

## THE DISCIPLES: COMPETING FOR POWER

As Peter, James, and John walk down the mountainside, they are still befuddled and confused. Along with the other disciples and followers of Jesus they begin the walk south into Galilee toward Capernaum. Enter into the narrative as Simon Peter offers guidance for this stretch of the pilgrimage in Mark 9:30-49 and 10:13-31.

Once again Jesus speaks of his betrayal, death, and resurrection. As they continue on the walk south, the disciples resist Jesus' announcements about his suffering and death by discussing who among them will get the most important places in the new order of the Messiah. Their conversation becomes heated and turns into an argument. After their arrival at Peter's house in Capernaum, Jesus asks them, "What were you arguing about on the way?" In response to their silence Jesus sits down and says to the disciples, "Whoever wants to be first must be last of all and the servant of all" (Mark 9:35). Then he invites one of the little children playing nearby in the house to come to him. He takes the child up in his arms, looks around at our gospel companions, and says:

> Whoever welcomes one such child in my name welcomes me, and whoever welcomes me, welcomes not me but the one who sent me. . . . If any of you put a stumbling block before one of these little ones who believe in me, it would be better for you if a great millstone were hung around your neck and you were thrown into the sea (Mark 9:37, 42).

Our assumptions about such words as *power* and *greatness* are shaken out of old thinking and doing by these words. The worth of children—these humble, receptive little ones among us—is lifted up before our gaze, along with the wonder of God's presence within the child, each child. We are invited to see—to really see. In that gaze of contemplation allow God to help you see children as God sees children. Children are believers; their hearts are open to wonder, to God, to Jesus. Jesus delivers a grave warning to any one who causes a child to doubt, to be unable to believe in God. He speaks not of a minor frustration but a holy rage against anyone who traps and blocks a child's mind and trust, thus robbing the child of his or her created freedom to trust in God.

These disciples are also "little ones"—children learning faith, learning the ways of the kingdom of heaven. When these followers of Jesus belittle one another in an attempt to prove one's superiority and greatness over the other, they are allowing their human lust for power to move into center place. Then they forget Jesus' patient and discerning guidance in naming their inward journey and outward calling. Jesus is directing their attention to the way of the kingdom: serving one another—being present, receptive, and helpful in their journey to become who God calls them to be. This way is greatness.

## JAMES AND JOHN: REJECTION OF OTHERS, DESTRUCTIVE RELIGIOUS ZEAL

Be present in these narratives of resistance as you read Mark 9:38-41 and Luke 9:44-50. John shifts the conversation. When Jesus directs John's attention toward learning to be a servant and welcoming little ones, John focuses on a confrontation he and the other disciples have experienced: "Teacher, we saw someone casting out demons in your name, and we tried to stop him, because he was not following us" (Mark 9:38). In reporting on this act of ministry, John seeks to divert attention away from Jesus' call to servanthood and humility and to declare the right to do ministry as legitimate only for those faithful who follow Jesus alongside this group of disciples.

In response Jesus draws their understanding back into the great hospitality of welcoming each one of "these little ones who believe in me" and replies to John and the others:

> Do not stop him; for no one who does a deed of power in my name will be able soon afterward to speak evil of me. Whoever is not against us is for us. For truly I tell you, whoever gives you a cup of water to drink because you bear the name of Christ will by no means lose the reward (Mark 9:39-41).

As spiritual director, Jesus opens up the narrow window of their understanding and invites these disciples to see all with whom Jesus stands in solidarity.

The walk south continues on through Galilee and then into Samaria. The people there, on hearing that Jesus was Jerusalem bound, refuse him hospitality. James and John—these Sons of Thunder—express their anger under the guise of prophetic and religious zeal: "Lord, do you want us to command fire to come down from heaven and consume them [as Elijah did]?" (Luke 9:54).

Jesus turns to them and rebukes them, directing them away from their fixation on getting their own way and toward what is driving them: "You do not know what spirit you are of, for the Son of Man has not come to destroy the lives of human beings but to save them" (Luke 9:54, footnote). Alvarez de Paz, a seventeenth-century spiritual guide, helps us understand the word *spirit* in this context: "A spirit is an internal impulse by which [one] feels [oneself] urged to do something."[5]

Throughout the scriptures and the literature of Christian spirituality, discernment of spirits is at work and central to the work of spiritual guidance. John, our gospel companion who came to recognize and struggle with the internal impulses of misdirected rage, tells the believers in his letter to "test the spirits to see whether they are from God" (1 John 4:1). It is this kind of discernment Jesus calls James and John to make as he invites them to see their anger and vengeance in the light of who he, the Son of Man, is and what he is about. He has not come to destroy lives but to save lives.

## REFLECTION

Invite the Holy Spirit to help you get in touch with the anger responses in your life:

- those places where you lack love and compassion for others
- those times when anger blocks your presence for God, for yourself, for others
- frustration with "little" people, tasks, what seems insignificant
- your need for control

Jericho is before them now, and then the uphill climb to Jerusalem. Simon Peter companions us as we leave the city. Enter into the narrative in Mark 10:46-52. Read prayerfully. Find your place among the people on the road.

# BARTIMAEUS: ICON OF SEEING

The Passover is near, and many people are on the road to Jerusalem. In addition, the highway is crowded because thieves stalk this route; it is safer to walk in a large group. Amid the bustle and talk of the crowd, a voice begins to cry out: "Jesus, Son of David, have mercy on me!" The yelling comes from Bartimaeus, a blind beggar, sitting by the roadside on the fringe of the crowd. People are angry and tell him to shut up. But Bartimaeus cries out even more loudly, "Son of David, have mercy on me!"

Jesus stands still and says, "Call him here."

The people nearest the beggar tell him, "Take heart; get up, he is calling you."

Bartimaeus throws off his cloak, springs up, and makes his way toward the voice of the one calling him. Kindly and with respect Jesus asks him, "What do you want me to do for you?"

Bartimaeus has no visions of grandeur or power. For years he has sat in that same spot and begged for money. But now he speaks a request that comes from his soul: "My teacher, let me see again."

Jesus responds and says, "Go, your faith has made you well."

As he walks alongside us, Bartimaeus becomes an icon. He can now see and follow Jesus. The disciples are still blind to what Jesus is trying to show them.

### REFLECTION

Spend some time within the gospel narrative. You are just outside the walls of Jericho.

- Where do you find yourself among the crowd?
- What is your response when you hear a blind beggar yelling for Jesus' attention?
- How do you feel when Jesus stands still and calls Bartimaeus?

After asking Bartimaeus what he wants Jesus to do for him, Jesus turns toward you and asks, "What do you want me to do for you?" Be in the presence of Jesus now and reflect on what he is asking you. Listen to the response of your soul and tell what you hear to Jesus. Listen for Jesus' response to what you say.

# Attending to Spiritual Guidance

## GATHERING AND SETTLING IN (15 MINUTES)

*Leader:* **In our last session together we reflected on how God tends the field of the soul—in the lives of those whom we serve in the church and in our own lives. We paid attention to the seasons of our lives when God is at work: when expectations are challenged, when we confront the impossible, when obedience in following Jesus is difficult and costly, and when our obedience is criticized.**

**As we begin our time together, let us pray.**

**Almighty God, you alone can bring into order the unruly wills and affections of sinners: Grant your people grace to love what you command and desire what you promise; that, among the swift and varied changes in the world, our hearts may surely there be fixed where true joys are to be found; through Jesus Christ our Lord, who lives and reigns with you and the Holy Spirit, one God, now and forever. Amen.[6]**

## MEDITATION (20 MINUTES)

Read the following passage twice.

> If any want to become my followers, let them deny themselves and take up their cross and follow me. For those who want to save their life will lose it. And those who lose their life for my sake, and for the sake of the gospel, will save it. For what will it profit them to gain the whole world and forfeit their life? Indeed, what can they give in return for their life? (Mark 8:34-37)

Let the group spend ten minutes in silent reflection, then spend another ten minutes in pairs, sharing your responses and your resistance to Jesus' call to cross bearing.

GROUP REFLECTION (1 HOUR 10 MINUTES)

1.  Review the various ways in which the disciples resist Jesus' telling them he would suffer. Their resistance reveals the issues they have with power, ambition, desire for authority, domination. In what way are these issues relevant to the lives of people in the group? (45 minutes)

2.  Working in pairs, talk with each other about ways in which you are seeking to respond to Jesus' call to childlike servanthood. (25 minutes)

CLOSURE (15 MINUTES)

End your time together in this session by walking into the narrative in Mark 10:46-52. After reading the passage slowly twice, allow a few minutes of silence for everyone to be present in the gospel story. Then read each of the reflection questions on pages 150–51, allowing one minute of silence for reflection between each question or statement.

*Leader:* **In preparation for our next time together, read chapter 11 and journal your responses to the Reflection sections. We will be celebrating the Lord's Supper, Eucharist, together. We may also consider whether we would wash one another's feet.**

Make the necessary arrangements about who will arrange the room space and provide the elements needed for serving the Lord's Supper. If foot washing will be included, make plans for that as well. The person ministering the communion may choose the order of service from his or her tradition and provide guidance for the group.

Close the session with a benediction.

# Chapter 11

## Learning to See as Jesus Sees

*Blessed are the peacemakers, for they will be called*
*children of God.—Matthew 5:9*

A storm of opposition mounts on the horizon as Jesus and his followers arrive in Bethany, two miles from Jerusalem. Judas is brooding in his
mind about crossing the line and defecting to the opposition. The high
priest, chief priests, scribes, and Pharisees are moving into collusion with
Sadducees and Herodians in their scheme to arrest Jesus with intent to
kill. But here in Bethany a family of friends offers a quiet oasis of rest and
hospitality. We are invited to join Jesus and our gospel companions at
table alongside Lazarus, Mary, and Martha. Listen as John sits with us
and shares his narrative in John 12:1-8. Mark 14:1-9 and Matthew 26:6-
13 also offer us memories of other similar table gatherings.

Martha has learned to lay aside the anxiety that could thrust her
into self-pitying and vindictive attack. Focused and at home with her gift
of hospitality and homemaking, she provides dinner for Jesus and his followers after their long walk south. Mary knows what lies ahead for Jesus

and has room at the table of her heart to hear him speak of his rejection, suffering, and death. Both sisters are thankful for Lazarus who is able to sit with Jesus at table. Healed from a fatal illness, their brother is now alive and well. Lazarus has known death, and he knows the journey back. He had heard Jesus call his name as he waited in the dark shadow of Hades, and the gates of death could not prevent his exodus. This brother and his two sisters have walked through the valley of death and have discovered that Jesus is the resurrection and the life (John 11).

## DO YOU SEE THIS WOMAN?

John remembers watching as Martha pays attention to serving food and then as Mary enters the room carrying a jar of oil of spikenard. Anger follows surprise among the disciples when she breaks open the jar and anoints Jesus' head and feet, then kneels to wipe his feet with her hair. The fragrance lingers in John's memory; he recalls the house being filled with the scent of spikenard. Judas, in charge of the common purse, voices their indignation: "Why was this perfume not sold for three hundred denarii, and the money given to the poor?"[1] The rest of the twelve now grumble at Mary. No one should be wasting costly spikenard, pouring it out as if it were common water from a well!

Jesus is not caught up in their reaction. Instead, he confronts their power play against Mary by telling them to "Leave her alone!" Then he offers some spiritual guidance: "She bought it so that she might keep it for the day of my burial. You always have the poor with you, but you do not always have me" (John 12:7).

In the various narratives about anointing, the twelve disciples appear to gang up in their reaction to women. This kind of group behavior still happens today when crowd mentality belittles or turns against an individual or group. Women can also find themselves caught up in such negative and destructive group behavior toward men. In becoming an advocate for Mary, Jesus invites the disciples to reflect on their attitude and behavior in a new way. Jesus directs their attention to the intent of Mary's gift by reframing her act in the light of his death, the pouring out of his own life.

Jesus leads these men—and we who are also present at the table of this narrative—to see with the eyes of the soul. Luke remembers an earlier encounter (Luke 7:36-50). A Pharisee named Simon had invited Jesus to eat with him. While they were at table, a woman entered the room. Luke does not give her a name, only a label: a "woman in the city, who was a sinner." Like Mary, she also brought a jar of ointment. Weeping, she bathed Jesus' feet with her tears, kissed them, and anointed them. Simon was critical and wondered why Jesus would allow such a woman to even touch him. Jesus responded by asking Simon, "Do you see this woman?" Of course Simon saw her. But Jesus was directing Simon to see with the eyes of the soul. This act of contemplation would allow God to reveal the woman for who she really was. Simon had seen this woman through the narrow lens of his religious righteousness, a lens that also filtered out the need for Jesus to receive the common rituals of welcome and courtesy. This woman had washed Jesus' feet, welcomed him with a kiss, and anointed him. Jesus *saw* this woman: a radical shift in attitude in a society where only men were counted while women and children were denied such recognition. The good news of the kingdom frees men to see and women and children to be seen and acknowledged for who they truly are—persons created in the image of God with gifts to offer.

Mary sees with the eyes of her soul—a contemplative gaze that is receptive to the suffering and death Jesus will embrace. In response, she anoints Jesus for his death and burial. The anointing is a ritual, speaking to the soul without words, a kind of knowing that draws our thinking and reason into a place of receptive transformation. Our gospel companions had not thought of giving something good and so costly to Jesus, just for him alone, out of love. But what is this talk about anointing him for burial? Is he going mad? Is Mary as crazy as he is? The disciples cannot grasp this yet nor fully understand. But Jesus is patient. He knows that the approaching storm is moving against their defenses of unbelief and denial and will change the way they see his suffering and death.

## REFLECTION

Pray for the Holy Spirit to open the eyes of your heart as you read John 12:1-8. Read the account twice and then enter into the narrative.

As you walk into the house, notice where you are in relation to Jesus, others. What are you doing? not doing? What is your response as you see Mary anointing Jesus' head and feet for his death and burial?

Spend some time contemplating Jesus, being present to Jesus.

In what way would you like to express your love to Jesus? in symbol? in words?

---

## JUBILATION AND GRIEF: ENTERING JERUSALEM

If our gospel companions have wondered when Jesus finally would declare himself as Messiah, they wonder no more. They are sure the day has finally come! Join the festive crowd and walk alongside Jesus as you read Mark 11:1-10 and Luke 19:37-48. As Jesus seats himself on a donkey, a crowd of people going up to Jerusalem gathers around, some spreading their jackets on the road and others cutting leafy branches from trees in the nearby fields to lay on the ground ahead of him. They begin shouting the prayer they know by heart from the Hebrew book of prayer, the Psalms.

> Save us, we beseech you, O LORD!
> O LORD, we beseech you, give us success!
> Blessed is the one who comes in the name of the LORD
> (Ps. 118:25-26).

Surrounded by the sound of chanted prayer beseeching God for success and salvation in overcoming military occupation, Jesus rides across the foothills of the Mount of Olives. He knows his life and work have been misunderstood and that no such political victory will happen. Deep in his heart he grieves over the inability of the people of Israel, God's own people, to see and embrace the presence of God among them.

The colt plods steadily along the road which curves right to run along the Kidron Valley for a short distance and then turns left, climbing toward the city. Jesus can see the Golden Gate ahead—entryway into Jerusalem and the temple. Overwhelmed with grief, he weeps, crying out to this beloved city and its people, "If you, even you, had only recognized on this day the things that make for peace! But now they are hidden from your eyes. . . . because you did not recognize the time of your visitation from God" (Luke 19:42-44). His cry recalls an earlier lament over the city: "How often have I desired to gather your children together as a hen gathers her brood under wings, and you were not willing!" (Matt. 23:37). This ancient city—and the temple Jesus embraces and knows as his Father's house—will soon be surrounded by enemies, attacked, and left in rubble.

Jesus is God among us—God coming to us offering peace, the way back home. The things that make for the peace Jesus brings will challenge and dismantle the way of the world and all that is not of God. According to the world's system, peace occurs when war ceases; the military might of one nation surpasses that of another; peace treaties are signed and national boundaries agreed on. God invites us to a deeper peacemaking initiated as we embrace the truth that we are at war with God, within ourselves, and with one another. Our journey back home begins when we accept God's way of peacemaking.

## REFLECTION

Take time to be present for God, simply to be with God. As you meet resistance, recognize it as being at war with God. Offer your resistance up to God. What are the things that make for peace in your life?

## BRINGING PEACE AND JUSTICE TO THE TEMPLE

Upon entering the Temple, Jesus sees crowds of people, pilgrims from many different countries standing in line, waiting to pay the Temple tax. Jews and converts to Jewish faith were required to pay one half-shekel around the time of the Passover. Jesus notes how the money changers charge a fee for this service, up to two-thirds of a working man's wage, and knows that worshippers from a distance especially could be exploited. Our gospel companions invite us to join them and offer guidance for our pilgrimage into the temple. Enter the narrative in Mark 11:15-19; 12:38-44; and Matthew 21:12-17.

Moved by compassion for the poor who come to pray and worship, and filled with love for all who seek God in this great court, Jesus moves with holy anger against those who place a stumbling block in the way of these children of God. He wades into the rows of tables, driving out vendors who sell doves and overturning the tables of the money changers. Then he turns and refuses access to persons carrying supplies across this holy space, saying, "Is it not written, 'My house shall be called a house of prayer for all the nations'? But you have made it a den of robbers."

In this moving act of advocacy Jesus reclaims this space for prayerful presence and directs our attention to who we are and in whose presence we gather when we enter sacred space.

People begin walking into the court now. Some grope their way along; others hobble on crutches; the blind and the lame make their way slowly toward Jesus. Here they are received, and here they are healed. A song begins to rise, its melody wafting clear and innocent into this newly hallowed sanctuary of prayer and healing. The children are singing praise to Jesus: "Hosanna to the Son of David!" But the chief priests and scribes refuse to embrace the wonders of healing and praise before them. Angry and fearful, they look for a way to kill Jesus, but their fear of the crowd keeps them in check.

Jesus continues to teach in the Temple. He warns the people against self-serving behaviors of the scribes which are designed to attract attention to their piety and prestige: special ways of dressing; demanding to be greeted in the market place; praying long prayers in order to be heard; sitting in places of honor in the synagogues and at banquets. While still on the banquet theme, Jesus goes on to expose these experts in the law of Moses for devouring widows' houses. Because of the scribes' selfish practice and behavior, widows are overlooked and denied the kind of social and financial support they need; they become the homeless in the Jewish society of Jesus' day.

Spiritual direction invites us to probe the motives for our behaviors and reflect realistically on how our choices affect the lives and well-being of others in the world. Our desire for prestige and attention is addictive. Jesus brings light into the dark areas of the self and its desires.

Our gospel companions lead us to another location within the Temple, the Women's Court. Jesus is observing people as they place money in the Temple treasury there. Many rich people give large sums. Then a very poor widow walks by and throws in two mites (worth about two-fifths of a cent), prompting Jesus to say:

> This poor widow has put in more than all those who are contributing to the treasury. For all of them have contributed out of their abundance; but she out of her poverty has put in everything she had, all she had to live on (Mark 12:43-44).

This woman stands at the opposite end of the socioeconomic line from the rich in her ability to contribute financially, but in the eyes of God she has given more than all the others. Spiritual direction helps us notice how following Jesus turns our economics upside down and shakes the contents of our pockets out onto the floor of God's presence. This poor widow also becomes an icon of Jesus. He has lived as a poor person with no income other than what is given him, and no place to live other than what others offer. Jesus has lived in simple trust in Abba and in others. Now he is about to give himself: all he has.

## REFLECTION

Recall different church buildings you have entered during your life.

- What kind of space within the building and within the worship service was made for prayer and attention to God's presence? Was there a room for prayer?

Pay attention to your experience of money.

- What was your family's attitude toward money when you were a child? What was the attitude of your parents, grandparents, others?
- What were you taught about earning, saving, spending, and giving money? These lessons may not have been verbal or explicit.
- What things were seen as valuable and worth owning and protecting? What does ownership mean to you now?
- When your income increases, what do you expect to do with the additional money?

- What is your attitude toward the poor? toward those who fall through the cracks of society?
- How do you respond to Jesus' teaching that giving money to provide for the poor is a spiritual discipline?
- In what ways do you practice poverty?

---

# STAYING AWAKE

Somehow we think that the world will get better if we work hard and try to improve our lives and the lives of others. There are rewards for hard, self-giving work. The dream beckons, but daily realities tell us that all will never be well. The disciples invite us into the narrative in Mark 13:1-36 and Matthew 24:9-14 as Jesus cuts through their dreams and hopes concerning a triumphal messianic intervention with hard news about the future. Pause and listen to Jesus' guidance remembered by Simon Peter and Matthew.

The signs of the end include wars, nations at odds with one another, earthquakes and famines; those who follow Jesus will suffer and will be betrayed. The signals that Jesus' return is close are dark and earth-shaking. In the midst of this dark and foreboding news Jesus places a light: The gospel first will be preached to all nations and then the end will come. Jesus will return and receive his own. Here Jesus offers spiritual guidance in the face of the demise of the world's system and the crumbling of what we know. In our postmodern world with its continual flux and uncertainty, shadowed by acts of terror and anxious attempts to ensure safety, Jesus offers guidance. We are to be faithful, to endure to the end, to proclaim the good news in life and in word to all nations, to stay awake and alert. We live in hope, a living hope that stretches far beyond the narrow passage of the time in which we live. We companion one another with patience and love and act as a presence for healing in the world.

## REFLECTION

What helps you to stay awake, expectant, and to serve faithfully as you wait and watch for Jesus' return?

———

# MARKING THE DAYS

All the gospel narrators call our attention to these final days of Jesus' life and later to the actual hours on the day of his death.

## WEDNESDAY

The hurricane is forming now. Two days before the Passover festival the chief priests and scribes meet in the palace of the high priest to discuss how they can arrest Jesus secretly and have him killed. In collusion with the dark forces at work within the religious leaders, Satan is also infiltrating the life of Judas Iscariot, who meets with the chief priests and Temple police to plan the betrayal of Jesus. Happy with Judas's cooperation, the religious leaders agree to pay him money for his services; the deal is made. Pause and ask the Holy Spirit to companion and help you as you live into these darker narratives in Matthew 26:1-5, 14-16; Mark 14:1-2, 10-11; John 12:20-36.

Judas does not recognize the secrecy required in turning against Jesus and the disciples as a sign that his actions are wrong. Just as our first parents in Eden were unaware of the deadly danger hovering along the dark path they had chosen, so Judas is blind to the demonic realities of his decision. Such are the ways of Satan and evil in the world. For good reason Jesus called Satan the father of lies. Judas begins to seek an opportunity for the religious leaders to arrest Jesus, a time when the crowd would not see or know what was happening.

Jesus does know what is about to happen. Again he tells his disciples, "The Son of Man will be handed over to be crucified." The hurricane is about to break over him and these, his beloved followers. As Jesus speaks about his death, he allows us entry into the sacred territory of his own soul: "Now my soul is troubled. And what should I say—'Father, save me from this hour?' No, it is for this reason that I have come to this hour. Father, glorify your name."

## THURSDAY

Passover is here. Jesus gathers with his disciples in a large upstairs room of a house in the city. As they eat they remember the great escape from slavery Yahweh had provided for their people. We are invited to join them at table. Ask the Holy Spirit to help you into the narrative as you read Mark 14:12-25; John 13:1-30; and Matthew 26:26-29.

Rescue from slavery dominates the forefront of the disciples' thinking. But Jesus is moving toward self-giving, the emptying of himself, humbling himself to become obedient to the point of death, even death on a cross (Phil. 2:8).

Jesus takes the bread and blesses it. Then he breaks it, gives it to the disciples, and says, "Take; this is my body" (Mark 14:22).

He takes a cup, and after giving thanks he gives it to them and says, "Drink from it, all of you; for this is my blood of the new covenant,[2] which is poured out for many for the forgiveness of sins. I tell you, I will never again drink of this fruit of the vine until that day when I drink it new with you in my Father's kingdom" (Matt. 26:27-29).

This is a Sinai moment (see Exod. 24:1-8). Jesus is announcing the new covenant, declaring the new thing God is doing. He would be the sacrifice, the Lamb of God; through the giving of himself we are made the people of God. This great work of God in the giving of God's Son stands at the center of all time, all history. This salvation event changes how the Hebrew Scriptures are to be read and understood. But the disciples miss the moment and begin to argue again among themselves as to which one of them is to be regarded as the greatest; who will receive places of prestige and power in the coming kingdom. Our gospel companions remember how Jesus enters their tight and constricted reality.

> Jesus, knowing that the Father had given all things into his hands, and that he had come from God and was going to God, got up from the table, took off his outer robe, and tied a towel around himself.

Then he poured water into a basin and began to wash the disciples' feet and to wipe them with the towel that was tied around him (John 13:3-5).

Rather than refuse their presence at the meal because of their repeated bouts of infighting, Jesus chooses a pastoral response of servanthood. Spiritual guidance is grounded and shaped by God's love.

## R E F L E C T I O N

Remember a time when someone responded to you with patience and loving servanthood rather than rejection and condemnation. How does such a Jesus-like response shape your own responses in ministry?

Jesus and his followers sing the Hallel from Psalms 115 to 118, then walk to the Mount of Olives where Jesus has stopped to pray during the week. Simon Peter asks us to come alongside him and the others in this dark night passage. Enter into the narrative as you read Mark 14:26-51; Luke 22:31-34, 39-46.

Jesus' words are somber: "You will all become deserters; for it is written, 'I will strike the shepherd, and the sheep will be scattered.' But after I am raised up, I will go before you to Galilee" (Mark 14:27-28).

Peter speaks up: "Even though all become deserters, I will not."

Jesus now seeks to explain to Simon and the other disciples how they also are being drawn into the great spiritual conflict about to unfurl.

> Simon, Simon, listen! Satan has demanded to sift all of you like wheat, but I have prayed for you that your own faith may not fail; and you, when once you have turned back, strengthen your brothers (Luke 22:31-32).

Here we discover the intent and heart of Jesus and God. Satan desires to destroy. God desires to help us, to strengthen us, to bring us into union with ourselves, with God, and with one another. Yes, something will fall apart. During the next few days the messianic and triumphal hopes and dreams carried within these followers of Jesus will be shattered and lost. They will know grief, doubt, loss, fear, unbelief, and guilt.

The process of loss masks the way of conversion, of transformation. Unless a grain of wheat fall in the ground and die, it remains alone. But if it dies, it bears fruit. At this moment Simon Peter and these followers cannot see that eventuality. Peter denies his own inner division, unaware of his own weakness. "Lord," he says, "I am ready to go with you to prison and to death!" (Luke 22:33). "Even though all become deserters, I will not" (Mark 14:29).

Jesus finally reveals the truth: "Truly I tell you, this day, this very night, before the cock crows twice, you will deny me three times" (Mark 14:31). But Peter continues in vehement denial: "Even though I must die with you, I will not deny you" (Mark 14:31). The rest of our gospel companions say the same.

Their walk brings them to the garden called Gethsemane on the slopes of the Mount of Olives. Jesus tells his companions how deeply grieved he is, even to death, and asks them to remain with him, to stay awake with him.

Three times he struggles in prayer, throwing himself prostrate on the ground as, again, great waves of self-protection pound against the house of his soul. "Abba, Father, for you all things are possible; remove this cup from me; yet, not what I want, but what you want." After each season of struggle and prayer, Jesus comes to the place where the disciples remain, but they are asleep, unable to stay with him in his grief and the awful decision to give himself over to be tortured and crucified.

Jesus knows the way of God, and he yields to this way—the way of the cross. He allows the hurricane to hit, to take his life. He has found the quiet center of God's will.

# Attending to Spiritual Guidance

## GATHERING AND SETTLING IN (15 MINUTES)

*Leader:* **In our last session together, we began by meditating on Jesus' call to cross bearing. In our group work we discussed the various ways in which the disciples resist Jesus' telling them that he would suffer and die. We looked at ways in which their resistance manifested itself: in issues with power, ambition, desire for authority, and domination. We discussed our own issues and resistance. In pairs we shared about how we are learning to respond to Jesus' call to servanthood.**

**As we begin our time together today, let us pray: Loving and providing God, Creator and Sustainer of all that is, help us by your Holy Spirit to open our hands and our hearts to you. Help us to let go of ownership, domination, and our selfish and prideful behavior. Cleanse and create a space within our souls for those who are poor and in need. Make us your servants, as you served us in Jesus Christ by washing our feet. In the name of Jesus, Amen.**

## MEDITATION (30 MINUTES)

Using the Reflection on pages 161–62, spend twenty minutes responding to the questions. Participants may have made entries in their journals. If so, they may review those. Be in the presence of God.

Ask the group to share responses to the Reflection with a partner. (10 minutes)

## PREPARATION (15 MINUTES)

Enter into the narrative in Luke 22:14-27. Find yourself in the upper room along with the disciples. The disciples were not present to Jesus or what he was offering at this table; be aware of the ways in which you avoid being present to the presence of God at times like these.

- What is your avoidance about?
- What comes to your attention?
- What is your response?
- In what ways are you struggling, resisting?
- In what ways are you saying, "Not my will but your will be done"?

Share responses to this reflection in the group. (15 minutes)

## GROUP WORSHIP AND REFLECTION (1 HOUR)

Using an order or service from your faith tradition, partake of the Lord's Supper/Eucharist together. You may also wish to wash one another's feet.

## CLOSURE

As you close, sing a hymn or song together.

Chapter 12

# Being Companioned
# When Everything Falls Apart

*Blessed are you when people revile you and persecute you*
*and utter all kinds of evil falsely on my account. Rejoice*
*and be glad, for your reward is great in heaven, for in*
*the same way they persecuted the prophets who were*
*before you. —Matthew 5:11-12*

## THURSDAY NIGHT

The storm breaks. Lanterns and fiery torches flare in the night; voices of the chief priests and Temple police trouble the quiet. Enter into this dark narrative as you read Matthew 26:47-56; Mark 14:43-51; Luke 22:47-53; and John 18:1-11.

Jesus' followers are ready to fight; they ask, "Lord, should we strike with the sword?" (Luke 22:49). Simon does not wait for a reply. He draws his sword and strikes out at the slave of the high priest, cutting off his ear. But Jesus already has fought his own battle, his revulsion against being handed over to evil, to mockery, flogging, and the slow agony of crucifixion and death. On the other side of that struggle and costly obedience he can see what is about to happen in the light of God's love and purpose. He has found the still point of God's presence and design at the center of the hurricane breaking upon him.

It is out of this spacious center that Jesus responds, first to Simon Peter, declining use of force: "Do you think that I cannot appeal to my Father, and he will at once send me more than twelve legions of angels? But how then would the scriptures be fulfilled, which say it must happen this way?" (Matt. 26:52-54; John 18:10). He turns then to Malchus, the wounded servant, and heals his ear. To his captors he offers spiritual guidance, revealing what drives their rejection and desire to kill him: the power of darkness.

The followers of Jesus admit later that they did not yet see or understand what Jesus was trying to show them. Stripped of their reliance on weapons to defend their Lord and themselves, they abandon Jesus and flee. They do not know any other way of defense and run from the threat of their own arrest and possible death. Jesus, however, does not abandon them. Although seized and arrested, Jesus holds his followers in his awareness, his prayer, his soul, and continues to offer them spiritual direction for this journey through terror, dark night, death, and resurrection.

## Purpose of the Dark Night Journey

Officers of the Temple police lead Jesus captive to the palace of the high priest. John and Peter decide to follow at a distance and gain entry into the lower courtyard. They invite us to join them where they stand in the warmth and flickering light of a charcoal fire. Enter prayerfully into their narrative of events as you read Mark 14:53-72; Luke 22:54-71; John 14:18-31; 18:12-27.

Determined to stay close to Jesus and loyal to this One whom he knows to be the Messiah, Simon positions himself in such a way as to see Jesus standing in the upper courtyard. He wants to hear what the Sanhedrin will say and do and how Jesus will reply. He knows Jesus deals with questions designed to trick and entrap him in an insightful and decisive way. Simon is not yet ready to deal with the warning Jesus has given him; he is not ready to own and wrestle with his own fears, his desires for power, and his pride. But Jesus does know Simon Peter. He sees what Simon needs to see and own.

The dark night journey enables us see what we have been blind to and to own what we have been avoiding. Sandra Cronk explains that we function with established ways of understanding the direction and purpose of our lives. These ways of understanding serve as structure and supports for the framework of our world, strong pillars that hold and order the shape of life.[1] Like the disciples, we tend to resist anything that threatens to dismantle these pillars. John of the Cross, a sixteenth-century spiritual director, says that during the dark night of the soul journey, the soul becomes a battlefield. God is present and at work, but we are unable to see and appreciate the collapse of that which has upheld us.[2]

Jesus sees the attack being mounted by Satan against Simon and the other disciples as a plan to split and divide them off against themselves and God. It is the nature of evil to hold up the lie from which it gains strength as a valuable truth, thus blinding us to the truth of the greater reality of God. Until we are able to see, we are blind to what God is doing. This transition from not seeing to seeing, from unawareness to awareness, can be a difficult and dangerous journey. But God intends this shift in knowing for these companions of Jesus—and for us.

Within these final chapters of the gospel narratives, the disciples invite us to companion them as this shift causes them to recognize and relinquish their own agenda for the Messiah and God's kingdom. This time of darkness, failure, and constant stripping away of all humanly based powers and strength is held and protected by God. Jesus knows that Satan has demanded to sift all of them like wheat, but Jesus has prayed protection into being (Luke 22:31-32).

> Holy Father, protect them in your name that you have given me, so that they may be one, as we are one. . . . I ask you to protect them from the evil one. They do not belong to the world, just as I do not

belong to the world. Sanctify them in the truth; your word is truth (John 17:11, 15-17).

## FACING THE WORST WITHIN OURSELVES

Two interrogations begin, one in the upper courtyard where Jesus stands before the Sanhedrin and the other on the lower level where Simon Peter and John stand around the fire along with servants of the high priest and Temple police.

In the first interrogation, the chief priests and council invite testimony of others against Jesus in order to put him to death. Jesus remains silent and does not respond to their testimony or the questioning of the high priest.

Meanwhile a servant girl of the high priest draws near in the courtyard below and notices Simon standing there. After looking at him more carefully in the light of the fire, she launches the second interrogation: "You also were with Jesus, the man from Nazareth" (Mark 14:67). Peter does not stay silent. He denies the observation, claiming he does not know or understand what she is talking about. Agitated, he leaves the group huddled around the warmth of glowing charcoal and walks to the forecourt nearby. Morning is about to dawn and a cock crows. The servant-girl says, "This man is one of them" (v. 69). Again Peter makes a denial. He refuses to own who he is in relation to Jesus.

In the upper courtyard Jesus remains silent. The high priest and court members have little to go on since the testimonies against Jesus prove false. The high priest decides to take another course of action and thinks up a way to make Jesus talk. "Are you the Messiah, the Son of the Blessed One?" he demands (Mark 14:61). Matthew remembers that the high priest forces an answer by putting Jesus "under oath before the living God" (Matt. 26:63). Jesus responds with a clear confession. He not only confesses who he is in relation to God but guides the court's attention to the greater reality of God's design for himself and hence for them: "I am; and 'you will see the Son of Man seated at the right hand of the Power,' and 'coming with the clouds of heaven'" (Mark 14:62; see Dan. 7:9-14).

But the high priest refuses to see or receive this prophetic truth. Instead, he tears his clothes and declares, "Why do we still need witnesses? You have heard his blasphemy! What is your decision?" The court condemns Jesus to death (Mark 14:63-64).

In the courtyard below the people standing around Peter move in closer and say, "Certainly you are one of them; for you are a Galilean" (Mark 14:70). At this point Peter begins to curse and then swears an oath of his own: "I do not know this man you are talking about" (v. 71). Peter hears the cock crow a second time. Instinctively he looks to the place where Jesus stands in the upper courtyard and sees Jesus turn to look toward him. This beloved rabbi remembers, does not turn away from this frightened, stubborn, and disillusioned disciple but stays present and waits as Peter remembers the guidance Jesus had given: "Before the cock crows twice, you will deny me three times." In that moment Simon Peter sees himself, his weakness, his fear, his betrayal. Broken and contrite at what he has just done and at what he recognizes within himself, he walks away into the night and weeps bitterly.

This is a dark place of stripping for Simon; his false bravado suddenly is gone, and his fear and betrayal lie underneath. However, this dark night is also a time of light. This is what Jesus was waiting for, has prayed for, and invites God's protection for: that Simon would see himself as Jesus sees him, would recognize his misguided passions regarding how the Messiah was to bring freedom and salvation, and would own his greed and appetite for boasting. This is love's patient and hospitable waiting within the ministry of soul care.

## REFLECTION

Where do you find yourself standing in the palace of the high priest? What do you experience as you are present in the narrative?

Reflect on times in your own life when you avoided confessing who you are in relation to Jesus. What are you aware of concerning your own willfulness, misguided passion, and weaknesses as a follower of Jesus? What is your response as Jesus sees you and all that is within you?

# FRIDAY

## VIGIL IN SUFFERING

At the entry door of Martin Chapel at Eastern Mennonite Seminary a small sign reads, "Please enter quietly." This little sign requests a certain intention, a quieting of our own inner noise and an appeal to be present. As we enter this part of the disciples' story, listen. Be receptive. Ask the Holy Spirit to help you to be present during this long vigil as Simon Peter, the women, and other gospel companions invite us to listen. Read Matthew 27; Mark 15:1-47; John 18:28–19:42; and Luke 23.

As morning breaks the chief priests order Jesus bound and arrange for him to be handed over to Pilate, the Roman proconsul. Another interrogation starts, and again Jesus does not speak in his own defense. Surprised, Pilate asks, "Do you refuse to speak to me? Do you not know that I have power to release you, and power to crucify you?" Jesus directs Pilate's attention to the greater reality of God and God's power rather than assisting his own defense: "You would have no power over me unless it had been given you from above" (John 19:10-11). It is within this greater reality of God's holding and power that Jesus allows himself to be handed over to the chief priests and scribes, to Pilate, and finally to the soldiers who flog, mock, and lead him—carrying the cross—to Golgotha to be crucified.

Spiritual guidance redirects our attention to God, whose power holds and protects our lives. While we trust that God will protect us from bodily harm and physical danger, Jesus calls us to a trust in God who holds us in the face of threat, fear, and death. Jesus has gone before us on this path when he walked to his death.

In the winter months of January and February, 1528, Hans Schlaffer prayed as he waited in prison to be executed for his faith in Jesus. A former priest who had come to a living faith in Christ, Hans was imprisoned in Austria along with some twenty other Anabaptist believers. In the face of certain death Hans remembers how Jesus prayed before his death and while he was dying; so, Hans brings his own journey to God. He prays for all fear to cease. "O almighty, eternal God, we recognize that we are weak and pray that you would strengthen us with the power of your Holy Spirit, that he would extinguish all human fear in us."[3]

But his prayer is not answered in the way he expects. Grief and fear haunt him, and Hans realizes he is "a poor brother in the Lord, a prisoner troubled unto death." He discovers comfort in solidarity with Jesus who agonized as his soul felt troubled unto death. In the following days and nights before his death Hans's prayer changes: "Therefore we pray, dear Father, that with your divine power you would keep us in all difficulties, offense, fear, and anxiety. . . . This is my comfort, O heavenly Father, in which Christ will strengthen and keep me with his power."[4]

## REFLECTION

The journey for those who follow Jesus encompasses suffering. This experience of suffering causes a crisis for the disciples but calls them to vigil and to deeper trust in God. In what way has suffering brought you into a place of deeper trust in God? In what way has God met you in suffering, offered guidance, and provided comfort?

## REMEMBERING

At the Last Supper, after taking a loaf of bread, giving thanks, breaking it, and giving it to his disciples, Jesus says, "This is my body, which is given for you. Do this in remembrance of me." In this partaking and remembering, time collapses, and we are invited to be present with these early disciples, and they with us, as Jesus offers his life for us.

Across the centuries Christian believers have entered into the practice of this spiritual discipline of remembering as a way of praying and staying centered throughout the day and as a way of receiving strength and consolation in the face of threat and terror. Hippolytus, bishop of the church in Rome from the end of the second and into the first decades of the third century, offers guidance for the practice of this spiritual discipline and will companion us in reflecting at the times and watches throughout this crucifixion vigil.

As we enter into the narrative of the crucifixion, our gospel companions will also be with us: Simon Peter, John, Matthew, Mary, Mary Magdalene, and women who had come up to Jerusalem with Jesus from Galilee. Simon Peter notes the time when Jesus is nailed to the cross.

*The Third Hour: Nine O'clock.* "And they crucified him, and divided his clothes among them, casting lots to decide what each should take. It was nine o'clock in the morning when they crucified him" (Mark 15:24-25). As Jesus is hoisted up on the cross which is then dropped with a jolt into the ground, he prays: "Father, forgive them, for they do not know what they are doing" (Luke 23:34). Our gospel companions remember Jesus' teaching: "Love your enemies and pray for those who persecute you, so that you may be children of your Father in heaven" (Matt. 5:44, 45). Here, before them, Jesus lives into his own teaching. Simon remembers asking how many times he should forgive a brother or sister who sins against him. Now he knows the heart of the matter is not counting but God and God's love and forgiveness. Later he would write to Christian believers who were suffering for their faith to tell them "love covers a multitude of sins" (1 Pet. 4:8).

Hippolytus offers spiritual guidance at the third hour to other believers who were experiencing stress and suffering, calling them to prayer across the day: "If you are at home at the third hour, pray and Praise God. But if you are elsewhere at this moment, pray to God in your heart. For at this hour Christ was nailed to the cross."[5]

Simon Peter directs our attention to the continual mocking and derision spoken by persons walking by: "Aha! You who would destroy the temple and build it in three days, save yourself, and come down from the cross!" (Mark 15:29-30). The chief priests and scribes also taunt him: "He saved others; he cannot save himself. Let the Messiah, the King of Israel, come down from the cross now, so that we may see and believe" (vv. 31-32). One of the two thieves crucified alongside Jesus joins the mockery: "Are you not the Messiah? Save yourself and us!" (Luke 23:39). The other thief challenges what he has just heard, calling his cynical partner to reflect on the reality of their situation and the reason they are condemned to die. Then he turns to Jesus and prays, "Jesus, remember me when you come into your kingdom" (Luke 23:42). God calls us to enter into remembering because God remembers. We are never forgotten. Jesus now turns to this man who is facing into his final journey and speaks words of comfort and reassurance: "Truly I tell you, today you will be with me in Paradise" (v. 43). This same Jesus who has heard his request will be there to meet him.

*The Sixth Hour: Noon.* The women who accompanied Jesus from Galilee and gave out of their own means toward his support are standing alongside us. They offer the gift of waiting and staying with him as Jesus hangs dying on the cross. Noon comes; the sun blazes high overhead. But suddenly the whole sky turns dark. Hidden from our gaze, the Lamb of God is bearing the sin of the world. The altar is the cross; his body given for us; his life poured out for us.

Hippolytus invites us to prayer:

> Pray likewise at the sixth hour. For while Christ was nailed to the wood of the cross, day was halted and a great darkness arose. At that hour, therefore, pray with great power, in imitation of him who prayed while all of creation was buried in darkness.[6]

*The Ninth Hour: Three O'clock.* Simon Peter remembers. He had also waited in the long, dark silence. Suddenly, at three o'clock he hears Jesus' voice. A lament sounds from the cross. Jesus laments, cries out to God, *"Eloi, Eloi, lema sabachthani?"* He is quoting a psalm.

> My God, my God, why have you forsaken me?
>> Why are you so far from helping me,
>> from the words of my groaning?
> O my God! I cry by day, but you do not answer;
>> and by night, but find no rest. . . .
>
> I am poured out like water,
>> and all my bones are out of joint;
> my heart is like wax;
>> it is melted within my breast;
> my mouth is dried up like a potsherd,
>> and my tongue sticks to my jaws;
>> you lay me in the dust of death
> (Ps. 22:1-2, 14-15).

Deeply planted within the souls of the Hebrews was permission to lament and cry out their doubts—"Why have you forsaken me?" "How long, O Lord? Will you forget me forever?"—in the presence of the One whom they experience as absent.

In his lament Jesus implicitly offers spiritual guidance: permission to grieve, to pour out the anguish and pain of our hearts. In times of sudden shock and loss, we cannot find words of our own to pray. September 11, 2001, was such a day. I found myself listening for words within my soul to lead the seminary community in a gathering of shock, grieving, and prayer but found none. Like other pilgrims, I turned to people in different times and places for words to speak and to pray—words offered in their lament and trial. The psalms with their many laments are such offerings.

Now that Jesus knows that all is finished, he says, "I am thirsty." A sponge full of sour wine is held up to his mouth on a branch of hyssop. When Jesus has received the wine, he announces: "It is finished! . . . Father, into your hands I commend my spirit" (John 19:30; Luke 23:46).

The great loving hands of Abba receive and hold Jesus as he breathes his last; his spirit leaves the house of his physical body to go home to God. Hippolytus invites our attention to this hour:

> At the ninth hour greatly lengthen your prayer and praise, imitating the souls of the just who bless the true God, who remembered his holy ones and sent his Son, the Word, to enlighten them.
>
> At this hour water and blood came from the pierced side of Christ, and (the Lord) gave light to the day as it declined, and brought it to evening. By thus beginning a new day at the hour when he began to fall asleep, he gave an image of the resurrection.[7]

*The Twelfth Hour: Six O'clock.* As evening draws close, two men step forward—disciples who have hidden in shadows of fear and secrecy but are now ready to stand alongside the others. Joseph of Arimathea, a member of the Sanhedrin who had not voted for Jesus' death, and Nicodemus, who had come to Jesus for a conversation about faith, offer a place for burial along with myrrh and aloes for anointing and linen cloths in which to wrap his body (John 19:39-40). Mary Magdalene, Mary the mother of Jesus, and the other Mary accompany Joseph and Nicodemus to the garden tomb, paying close attention to where Jesus is buried.

As sabbath begins, the women rest and wait. Their vigil continues. The other disciples hide in a locked room, fearing for their lives.

# Attending to Spiritual Guidance

### GATHERING AND SETTLING IN (15 MINUTES)

*Leader:* **In our last gathering we responded to reflection questions about spaces for prayer in our church buildings, in our meetings, and in worship and to questions about our attitude toward money. We celebrated the Lord's Supper together after spending time in reflection and preparation. And, just as Jesus and the disciples sang a hymn before leaving the upper room, we also closed our time at the communion table by singing a hymn.**

### MEDITATION (20 MINUTES)

Arrange for the group members to take turns reading Mark 14:32–15:47. This description of Jesus' prayer vigil, the arrest, trial, betrayal, flogging and mocking, and crucifixion, is divided into nine parts (see below). Pause for one minute following the reading of each scripture, allowing time for prayerful presence and reflection. Have nine candles lit and arranged on the worship center. After the reading of each of the nine sections, extinguish one of the candles until the room is in darkness for the time of final reflection. You may choose to have the group sing a hymn or refrain at certain points during the readings.

> **First reader:** Mark 14:32-34 (Pause, silence); Mark 14:35-38 (Pause, silence); Mark 14:39 (Pause, silence)
>
> **Second reader:** Mark 14:40-52 (Pause, silence)
>
> **Third reader:** Mark 14:53-65 (Pause, silence)
>
> **Fourth reader:** Mark 14:66-72 (Pause, silence)
>
> **Fifth reader:** Mark 15:1-15 (Pause, silence)
>
> **Sixth reader:** Mark 15:16-20 (Pause, silence)
>
> **Seventh reader:** Mark 15:21-24 (Pause, silence)

**Eighth reader:** Mark 15:25-32 (Pause, silence); Mark 15:33-41 (Pause, silence)

**Ninth reader:** Mark 15:42-47 (Pause, silence)

GROUP REFLECTION (1 HOUR 10 MINUTES)

This chapter seeks to capture the movement of the dark night journey, those times in our lives when the structures and supports of our life are dismantled and no longer support us. The term *dark night* refers to the experience of not being able to see or understand what is happening or where this journey will lead. As Jesus walks steadily toward suffering and death, the disciples feel fear and terror. Only later will they know what this death journey was about. Until then, they are "in the dark." Using chapter 12 for reference, discuss in your group the dark night experience of the disciples, especially Simon Peter. The following questions may prompt discussion. (30 minutes)

- What kind of pillars or supports are crumbling?
- What are they afraid of?
- In what way do they suffer?
- In what ways do they run away, and in what ways do they stay present to what is happening?
- What changes for them during this dark night?
- Can you describe what this change felt like for Simon Peter?
- How did Jesus guide his followers during this dark night?

*Leader:* Spend twenty mintues in solitude now to reflect on a dark night experience in your own life journey. Get in touch with the following:

- the circumstances that thrust you into this dark night journey, what experience of loss you encountered
- your own personal reaction within this season

Bring your experience into the light of the crucifixion narrative and the dark night experienced by Jesus' followers.

- What has God/Jesus been saying that the disciples—and you— have been unable to hear?
- What do you notice about Jesus' response to loss and abandonment that is helpful to you?

- **In what way is this section of the gospel narrative helpful to you in your own dark night experience?**

After the time of solitude, lead the group in sharing dark night experiences with one another for thirty minutes.

## CLOSURE (15 MINUTES)

*Leader:* **In preparation for our final session, read chapter 13 and respond to reflection questions in your journal.**

If your group will not be meeting again after concluding this study and attending to spiritual guidance together, decide on how you would like to bring closure and celebrate this experience of learning together.

As you close in prayer, invite each person present to hold a lit candle—symbolizing the presence of the Spirit of Jesus with you in whatever you are experiencing in your lives and ministries at this time.

# Chapter 13

# Rewriting Our Story
# in Light of the Great Story

*Blessed are those who mourn,*
*for they will be comforted.—Matthew 5:4*

$\mathcal{F}$ollowing Jesus does not mend the gap in which we live or rewrite the flawed content of our story in an instant. Our narrative is so deeply embedded within our soul and being that usually we are unaware of its presence and influence. During the three years in which Jesus companioned the disciples—both men and women—he paid careful and discerning attention to how their distorted understandings blocked them from embracing the grace and freedom of God's loving rule present among them. His suffering, death, burial, and resurrection speak of how God rewrites our story by offering us the Great Story of God's love and self-giving.

In the days following the resurrection, we find Jesus at work helping his followers attend to this rewriting in light of the Great Story. Our gospel companions invite us into three narratives, each with an invitation to receive spiritual direction from Jesus as he cares for growth in faith, hope, and love.

## SPIRITUAL DIRECTION FOR GROWTH IN FAITH

Dawn creeps across the sky as we enter the first narrative. A new day begins. Ask the Holy Spirit to open the eyes and ears of your soul to see and to know as Mary, Mary Magdalene, Matthew, and John companion us in Matthew 28:1-10; John 20:11-29; and Luke 24:10.

Mary, Joanna, Mary Magdalene, and some other women come early, wondering who will roll away the stone from the tomb. They desire to complete the task of anointing and wrapping Jesus' body for burial. This need to see and give proper burial to Jesus' body is part of grieving; the traditional rituals hold the women steady at a time when all else seems to have fallen apart. To their shock and amazement, an angel appears and rolls away the very thing they had been worrying about. To their further surprise, this heavenly visitor has a message to give them personally:

> Do not be afraid: I know that you are looking for Jesus who was crucified. He is not here; for he has been raised, as he said. Come see the place where he lay. Then go quickly and tell his disciples, "He has been raised from the dead, and indeed he is going ahead of you to Galilee; there you will see him." This is my message for you (Matt. 28:5-7).

This last piece of the message gives us a clue as to how God communicates the new story, shaping the message in a way that fits the understanding and receptivity of the receivers. Being with our gospel companions during these earthshaking days illumines the care and individuality with which God guides these women and men to shift the foundation and create new pillars for rewriting their story. Here we catch a glimpse of the servanthood of God on our behalf: God pays attention specifically to the event and to how the message is communicated. Such careful communication marks God's guidance.

As these women turn to leave the empty grave, they feel both fearful and joyful. The old story is gradually giving way to the new. Quite suddenly, as they are running to deliver their astounding message, they see Jesus coming to meet them.

"Greetings!" he says in welcome. In their joy and relief, they bend low and worship, holding on to Jesus' feet. They do not know that their need to hold on to his physical presence is a deeply imbedded fear response also connected with their need to feel accepted. The interior structures of the women's false selves come into play.

Ever since Eden the pillars of the false self have written a distorted desire for closeness and acceptance into the storied experience of women. The false self creates a delusion: "I am only secure if you are close, and I exist—I am somebody—if you choose to stay close to me." These human fears of losing a sense of self and of being abandoned are the shaky pillars of the false self and its belief systems for both men and women. Women tend to depend on others and often will negate their own true sense of self. The work for women, then, is learning to love and embrace their self and personhood, discerning the presence of the false self and its attachment needs. While childhood trauma and abandonment can work in collusion with the false self's dynamics—its attachment and identity needs—I am speaking of something more basic. The root is contaminated with evil and the lie spun by Satan like a powerful web in Eden (Gen. 3:1-7).

Ann Belford Ulanov speaks to this fundamental misperception. A Jungian therapist and spiritual director, Ulanov recognizes that even when a woman experiences a growing consciousness of being valued for who she is, she can be tempted to make it nothing by not knowing about it, by not keeping this truth in her consciousness. Ulanov describes evil as the kind of driving force that is present and at work before any experience of abandonment or loss, a power that cuts things off at the root so that nothing can grow.[1]

Jesus cuts through the power of the lie and the shadowy attachments of the false self in two ways. First, he speaks to the fear in these women, naming the source of their need to hold on to him. Second, he empowers them as women by accepting them as human beings created in the image of God and calling them to minister: "Go and tell my brothers to go to Galilee; there they will see me" (Matt. 28:10). The women's restored faith energizes their feet as they run to announce the good news.

Mary Magdalene returns to the grave, however. She is not able to let go of the story that has sustained her over these last few years. She already has done a major rewriting of her story—written boldly with the person of Jesus present and alive on each page. He is the central pillar of her new life. Jesus had received her as she came, and with loving discernment and holy power he freed her from the demons haunting her lonely and compulsive existence. Rewrite her story again? Her trauma blocks all thought of the future and possible change. She is unable to believe. Bending down, her eyes full of tears, she looks into the tomb once more, as if checking to see whether she had missed seeing Jesus' body the first time. No, he wasn't there, but someone else was. Two angels sit where Jesus' body had been laid. Gently they ask her, "Woman, why are you weeping?" (John 20:13).

"They have taken away my Lord, and I do not know where they have laid him," Mary responds (v. 13). It was one thing for Jesus to be crucified; it is another for his body to be gone—such profound absence and emptiness. The empty tomb pulls to the surface her experience of being lost and alone in the dark shadows of demonic control; she turns away from the angels and the empty grave. A man stands in the garden. It is Jesus, but she cannot recognize him. Jesus asks her the same question, "Woman, why are you weeping?" and then, "Whom are you looking for?"

These gentle, open-ended questions (John 20:15) invite Mary Magdalene to explore the layers of her grief, to pay attention to the source of her tears, and to speak about her loss. Just as she does not seem to have been aware of the presence of angels, Mary Magdalene is not aware of this man's identity. Profound grief can blur our perception of reality and hem us in with an inability to see, which—at least for a time—protects from the enormity of pain we are experiencing. Mary Magdalene continues to explain away these signs and messages from God and assumes that this man is the gardener. Even though grief clouds her vision, Mary is still searching for Jesus. At this point Jesus chooses to say her name,

"Mary!" (John 20:16). Like Lazarus who, though bound by death and the grave clothes, could hear his name called by Jesus and respond to that call, so Mary knows the sound of that voice!

Whenever we offer spiritual guidance, we are invited to recognize our dependence on the power and authority of Jesus' calling the person out from the false and oppressive structures supported by the pillars of that individual's particular story. Mary hears her name and she recognizes who this man is standing before her. Not only does Jesus free her to hear, but he also opens her eyes to see. "Rabbouni!" she exclaims, as she reaches out to clasp hold of him.

We may be spiritual companions to those who seek, but finally it is God who reveals God's self and who helps a person to know who Jesus is. Although we can point to God and assist a person to pay attention to the presence and person of Jesus, we cannot make someone see. This is the work of the Holy Spirit: to open the eyes of the soul to the great reality of God's gracious presence and rule. With sensitivity and care the Spirit knows when a person is ready to see. Jesus knows the moment in which to speak Mary Magdalene's name, and she is able to hear and to believe. He is about to ascend to his Father and to her Father, to his God and to hers. Just as he has a future, she does also. He calls her to live into faith and trust rather than be held back by her past. Finally she is also able to go and tell the other disciples what she has seen and heard. Her story is being rewritten.

Disillusioned, the disciples huddle in their collective and separate grief in a room in Jerusalem, the doors locked because they fear the religious authorities. If Jesus had been arrested and crucified on charges of saying he was King of the Jews, what might happen to them, his closest followers? When they hear what the women say about the resurrection, the angels' message, and seeing Jesus, they are unable to believe what they hear. Not yet.

Evening comes. Suddenly they realize that someone else is standing among them, saying, "Peace be with you" (John 20:19). This same One shows them his hands and his side—the wounds of crucifixion and a sword's piercing.

A week later Thomas is among the disciples when Jesus appears again, entering the room in a way that defies human understanding. Jesus extends the same greeting, "Peace be with you," and a prompting to Thomas to see and to touch his hands and side. Jesus' presence with the disciples and his invitation for them to see the wounds help our gospel companions make a shift in their faith. They are beginning to rewrite their story.

These followers are drawn now into a new solidarity with Jesus. Just as God sent him into the world, so Jesus sends them. And just as the Holy Spirit came upon Jesus as he began his ministry, so Jesus breathes upon them and says, "Receive the Holy Spirit. If you forgive the sins of any, they are forgiven them; if you retain the sins of any, they are retained" (John 20:22-23). With these words Jesus not only confers a God-given authority upon his followers (compare Mark 2:7) but also reminds them of what kingdom authority is about: the freedom and compassionate power to forgive. At the heart of his teaching, his life, and his sacrificial death shines this release from bondage. Matthew, the former tax collector, remembers well: Jesus came to call not the righteous but sinners (Matt. 9:13). All of them could call to mind the prayer Jesus taught them: "[F]orgive us our sins, for we ourselves forgive everyone indebted to us" (Luke 11:4).

One mark of the Holy Spirit's presence upon and within the disciples will be their response to sin. Forgiveness is not automatic or easy but to be given. At the same time, they receive guidance concerning the possibility of withholding forgiveness. Our responses have eternal implications and shape the kingdom. We are called to forgive just as we have been forgiven.

## REFLECTION

In what ways are you aware of growth in faith—those times when you turn to God in trust and dependence?

For women: In what ways does your growth in faith empower you to embrace your strength and identity, to embrace the call of God on your life to speak the Good News—in your being and in your acts of ministry?

For men: In what ways do you turn to God in simple trust when you feel disempowered, weak, unable? How are you becoming receptive to God's presence and help in these times?

---

## Spiritual Direction for Growth in Hope

On the afternoon of that same day Cleopas and another disciple decide to walk home to Emmaus, about seven miles from Jerusalem. Cleopas and his companion draw us into the narrative in Luke 24:13-49 as they walk and talk with each other, going over all the things that happened in the last few days. While in deep conversation, Jesus comes near and walks with them. But like Mary Magdalene, they are unable to recognize him. After a while Jesus asks, "What are you discussing with each other while you walk along?"

They stand still, their faces marked by grief. For a moment these disciples are silent, and then Cleopas asks this stranger a question of his own: "Are you the only stranger in Jerusalem who does not know the things that have taken place there in these days?" (Luke 24:18).

"What things?" Jesus asks. This is a kind, open-ended question, encouraging these two sorrowful disciples to explore their own story and experience.

"The things about Jesus of Nazareth. . . . We had hoped that he was the one to redeem Israel" (Luke 24:19-21). Here they are able to name what is so profoundly wrong with events that took place: They had hoped Jesus was the one to rescue their people from Roman occupation. Now he is dead and with him their own hopes have died also.

Jesus hears them speak of their loss of hope and now discerns the cause for their soul sickness, their slowness of heart to believe, and their inability to embrace suffering in the Great Story of God. "Was it not necessary that the Messiah should suffer these things and then enter into his glory?" (Luke 24:26) He leads them through the scriptures in his response, enlarging their grasp of the sacred story and thus helping them to rewrite their own as their hearts burn with renewed hope.

When these two ask the gifted and insightful stranger to eat with them, Jesus does what he often does. He comes as guest in response to our invitation and then becomes host at the table. He takes bread, blesses and breaks it, and gives it to them, and they recognize him. Energized and full of joy, they walk the seven miles back to Jerusalem and announce the good news. While they are in the midst of telling, Jesus appears, speaking words of guidance and help to these troubled followers. And then he leads them through the scriptures in the same way that he had done for Cleopas and his companion earlier that afternoon.

Spiritual direction pays attention to hope and loss of hope within the storied experience of another. In this way we become story listeners, always alert to where hope exists and where despair lies within a person's story. If we are unable to name and be present to our own experiences of loss and despair, of pillars that formerly felt secure crumbling, we will find it hard to stay present to the story of others. Simon Peter, along with the rest of our gospel companions, learned to rewrite his own limited story and to say, "Blessed be the God and Father of our Lord Jesus Christ! By his great mercy he has given us a new birth into a living hope through the resurrection of Jesus Christ from the dead" (1 Pet. 1:3).

## REFLECTION

Look back over your life and become aware of those times when your hopes were disappointed and you felt disillusioned and disempowered.

- In what ways did God restore hope in your life?
- In what ways are you rewriting your story?

## SPIRITUAL DIRECTION FOR GROWTH IN LOVE

It is time for the disciples to return to Capernaum, to their homes beside the Lake of Galilee. Jesus has told the disciples he would be waiting to meet them there. Simon Peter and John invite us to join them as dawn spills its light across the dark waters of Lake Galilee. Enter the narrative prayerfully as you read John 21.

A charcoal fire glows on the shore. Our gospel companions have been fishing all night—a fishing expedition initiated by Peter. Jesus calls to them, asking if they have caught any fish. They have caught nothing. "Cast the net to the right side of the boat, and you will find some," he replies (v. 6). So they cast the net and find it too full to haul in. John now recognizes the One standing on the shore: "It is the Lord!" he shouts. With sudden joy and relief, Simon grabs his tunic, jumps into the lake water, and swims to shore. The smell of fish roasting on the charcoal fire greets him as he wades out of the water, along with a kind proposal: "Come and have breakfast," Jesus says (v. 12).

Here Jesus is host as well as cook. He comes to these men in this familiar place beside the lake, offering comfort for body and for soul. After breakfast he asks Simon Peter to walk with him along the shore. Jesus opens the conversation: "Simon son of John, do you love me more than these?" Simon replies, "Yes, Lord; you know that I love you" (v. 16).

Jesus is not inquiring about strength. He does not mention Simon Peter's betrayal. He does not condemn this man who is first to speak, often first to initiate action, and who repeatedly admits how much he falls and fails. This is a conversation about loving.

Jesus has chosen to care for the setting of this exchange in a way that evokes this disciple's memories of his fear and weakness, those times when Simon Peter caught a glimpse of his interior self. Whereas Jesus empowers women to notice and embrace their strength of identity, he calls men to discover and own what could be perceived as weakness within themselves. Jesus launches women into the adventure of individuation even as he sends them on the outward journey of ministry. He invites men to turn toward the inward journey of intimacy and vulnerability, even as they too are called to outward ministry.

Jesus asks this disciple a second time, "Simon son of John, do you love me?" There is no mention of Peter here, rather an invitation to Simon to remember his human origin, to own his humanity rather than get caught up in the facade of a rock-like leader. "Yes, Lord; you know that I love you," he replies.

"Tend my sheep," Jesus says in response. Then Jesus asks again, a third time, "Simon son of John, do you love me?" This insistent questioning finally gets through Simon's tough exterior and finds its way into the great heart and soul of this man. Peter begins to feel pain: the pain of not always being able to succeed—even as a fisherman; the pain of knowing he did not measure up to gracious holiness that permeated the being of Jesus; the pain of knowing he had boasted of great loyalty to the Messiah but at the hint of threat had denied knowing him. Finally, he is able to stay with his pain and just to be with himself—human, weak, fallible, limited, sinful. Jesus had stayed with him all across these years and walks beside him now—just as he is. "Lord, you know everything; you know that I love you."

Yes, Jesus does know everything about him. Now Simon Peter is beginning to know himself even as he is known. He has come home to himself and home to God in a new way. A new intimacy is emerging within his mind and being. This self-awareness, an inner strength to stay present to himself rather than adopt a strong but false front, would enable him to be present to God and to do what Jesus calls him to do: "Feed my sheep."

Bernard of Clairvaux, an abbot in the Cistercian order during the twelfth century, offers spiritual guidance about loving.[2] He says that first we love ourselves for our own sake. While this kind of love can be self-centered and narcissistic, it is needful for us to love and be protective and caring of ourselves. When we begin to realize that we need someone beyond our self, we begin to seek God. At this point we experience God as useful and necessary. Our love begins to change and grow; we love God because God provides what we need. Simon Peter had come to know Jesus in this way—as the Messiah who fed the multitude, stilled storms on the lake, who healed the sick. He also expected Jesus to claim the throne of David and restore the nation of Israel. When the latter expectation did not become reality, Simon's love and loyalty faltered. He had not yet been able to grow in his experience and practice of loving God because of who God is—not just because of what God is able to do for him.

Later Simon Peter would be tending the flock, feeding the sheep of God's pasture. He would be able to speak of love and the enormous capacity of love to embrace and to stay with the weakness and sin within people. He would advise followers of Jesus above all to maintain constant love for one another, for love covers a multitude of sins. To be hospitable to one another without complaining. Like good stewards of the manifold grace of God, to serve one another with whatever gift each person has received.

## REFLECTION

We have a tendency to look back over our lives and notice where we have sinned or fallen short of God's call on our lives. Our gospel companions remember the many times when Jesus noticed and named the presence of faith and love in people's lives. In the New Testament letters we discover the writers affirming the faith, hope, and love being lived out in the lives of believers in the churches. Formulated in the seventeenth century by Ignatius of Loyola, the Consciousness Examen is a spiritual discipline that offers guidance as we reflect on the presence and activity of faith, hope, and love in our daily living.

*Preparation.* Ask the Holy Spirit to help you see your life as God sees your life.

*Reflection.* Look back over the last day (or week). Let the events unfold and pass before you. What emerges? What persons or events stand out for you? For what are you thankful? For what are you least thankful? What attitudes do you notice within yourself?

- anxiety, anger, sadness, fear, guilt, hostility, grief, other?
- faith: responding to God?
- hope: responding in hope in the face of difficulties?
- love: responding to yourself and to others?

Where are these attitudes taking you?

- toward God, yourself, others?
- away from God, yourself, others?

Be in the presence of God now. Bring your needs, your confession, your petitions. Know that you are heard, loved, forgiven, and restored. Bring your gratitude and simply rest in the presence of God.

# Attending to Spiritual Guidance

## GATHERING AND SETTLING IN (15 MINUTES)

*Leader:* **In our last meeting we entered the narrative of the crucifixion and spent time reflecting on the dark night journey in the lives of the disciples and in our own experience. Today we will open our time together by practicing the Consciousness Examen together. Let us pray together: Loving and sustaining God, by your Holy Spirit open the eyes of our souls to see what you desire for us to see and the ears of our hearts to hear what you want us to hear. Help us to see our lives as you do. In the name of Jesus, our Savior and Lord, Amen.**

## MEDITATION (30 MINUTES)

Using the prayer guide in the Reflection section at the end of chapter 13, practice the Consciousness Examen together. As leader, allow pauses of one minute for personal reflection between each line of the guidance instructions. Allow a longer pause of three minutes for people to pray their needs, confession, petitions; and a pause of three minutes for people to express gratitude and to rest in God's presence. (20 minutes)

Invite the group to form pairs and listen to each other's experience of practicing the Consciousness Examen. (10 minutes)

## GROUP REFLECTION (1 HOUR)

Take time now as a group to reflect on the ways you have learned to listen, to be prayerfully present to one another and to persons in your sphere of ministry.

Spend fifteen minutes posing the following questions to participants and then forty minutes sharing your responses with one another as a group.

In what ways are you growing in your capacity to

- be present to God? cooperate with God?
- be aware of resistance to God?
- listen to the experience of another or within a group?
- notice God's presence and work within the experience of your partner? the group? the congregation (or place of ministry)?

What responses do you notice emerging within yourself as you listen to others share their personal or spiritual experiences?

- compassion/empathy
- seeking to hear and understand
- trying to fix
- offering advice, preaching
- boredom, distance; turning your mind to other agenda
- able to stay with the experience of the person sharing without rehearsing how to reply
- becoming more aware of the different ways in which God is present and the Holy Spirit active in another
- being prayerfully present
- allowing silence, turning to God in prayer when needing help

What else have you learned in this study?

## CLOSURE (15 MINUTES)

*Leader:* As we end this journey together, our gospel companions call us into the narrative one more time. They invite us to join them on the mountain again, near to the Lake of Galilee. Jesus has asked them—and us—to meet with him there. Matthew guides us into the narrative: "Now the eleven disciples went to Galilee, to the mountain to which Jesus had directed them. Jesus was waiting for them there. When they saw him, they worshiped him; but some doubted." We are in the narrative now, on the mountain. And Jesus is waiting for us there.

(Pause for one minute.)

Jesus comes and says to the disciples and to us:

LEADER: All authority in heaven and on earth has been given to me.

GROUP MEMBERS: Remember, authority is given to Jesus. A gift given.

LEADER: Go therefore and make disciples.

GROUP MEMBERS: Make disciples as Jesus made disciples. What are you looking for? Come, follow me, and I will make you fish for people. What do you want me to do for you?

LEADER: Baptizing them in the name of the Father and of the Son and of the Holy Spirit.

GROUP MEMBERS: Remember God's words to us: You are my beloved child, in you I am well pleased.

LEADER: Teaching them to obey everything that I have commanded you.

GROUP MEMBERS: Help people to learn to listen, to listen deeply. Companion them as they learn to express in their lives what they are knowing in their heart and soul.

LEADER: And remember

GROUP MEMBERS: and remember

LEADER: And remember, I am with you always, to the end of the age.

GROUP MEMBERS: Remember, I am with you always, to the end of the age.

TOGETHER: Remember, I am with you.

(Time of silence.)

Close with a benediction and a blessing on each person. Be present to one another as you bring closure and bless one another before departure.

# NOTES

## INTRODUCTION

1. Jack Dean Kingsbury, *Matthew as Story*, second edition (Philadelphia: Fortress Press, 1988), 2.

2. Thomas C. Oden and Christopher A. Hall, *Mark* in Ancient Christian Commentary on Scripture: New Testament II, ed. Thomas C. Oden (Downers Grove, Ill.: InterVarsity Press, 1990), xxi-xxiv.

## CHAPTER 1

1. Margaret Guenther, *Holy Listening: The Art of Spiritual Direction* (Boston: Cowley Publications, 1992), 9.

2. Ann Ulanov, *The Wisdom of the Psyche* (Cambridge, Mass.: Cowley Publications, 1988), 130.

3. Ben Campbell Johnson, *Speaking of God: Evangelism as Initial Spiritual Guidance* (Louisville: Westminster/John Knox Press, 1991), 13.

4. In these and later excerpts from conversations I have changed informational content to protect the confidentiality of persons who do come for spiritual direction. However mixed the composite, the facts are true to their experience.

5. Janet Ruffing, *Uncovering Stories of Faith: Spiritual Direction and Narrative* (Mahwah, N.J.: Paulist Press, 1989), 17, 18.

6. Martin Thornton, *The Rock and the River* (1965), 141–42; quoted in Kenneth Leech, *Soul Friend: The Practice of Christian Spirituality* (San Francisco: Harper & Row, Publishers, 1977), 35.

7. Katherine Marie Dyckman and L. Patrick Carroll, *Inviting the Mystic Supporting the Prophet: An Introduction to Spiritual Direction* (Ramsey, N.J.: Paulist Press, 1981), 20.

8. Kenneth Leech also speaks of this mutuality of seeking in *Soul Friend*, 34.

9. Thomas Merton, *Spiritual Direction and Meditation* (Collegeville, Minn.: The Liturgical Press, 1960), 16, 17.

10. William A. Barry and William J. Connolly, *The Practice of Spiritual Direction* (San Francisco: Harper & Row Publishers, 1982), 8.

11. Tilden Edwards, *Spiritual Friend: Reclaiming the Gift of Spiritual Direction* (New York: Paulist Press, 1980), 94–98.

12. Sara Wenger Shenk, "Toward an Anabaptist Theory of Education" (Ed.D. diss., Union Theological Seminary, Richmond, Virginia, 1998), 243.

13. Damien Isabell, *The Spiritual Director: A Practical Guide* (Chicago: Franciscan Herald Press, 1976), 9, 12–14.

14. Dyckman, *Inviting the Mystics,* 20.

CHAPTER 2

1. E. Rozanne Elder, "William of St. Thierry: Rational and Affective Spirituality," *The Spirituality of Western Christendom*; quoted in Tilden Edwards, *Spiritual Friend,* 235-36.

2. Dom Francois Vandenbrouke, "Laity and Clergy in the Thirteenth Century," *A History of Christian Spirituality,* ed. Louis Bouyer (New York: Desclee, 1970), vol. II, pt. 2; quoted in Edwards, *Spiritual Friend,* 236.

3. Leech, *Soul Friend,* 35.

4. Ibid., 35, 36.

5. Edwards, *Spiritual Friend,* 17.

6. Ibid., 6.

7. Ulanov, *Wisdom of the Psyche,* 118.

8. Johnson, *Speaking of God,* 12.

9. Eugene H. Peterson, *Working the Angles: The Shape of Pastoral Integrity* (Grand Rapids, Mich.: Wm. B. Eerdmans Publishing Co., 1987), 151.

10. Calvin E. Shenk, *Who Do You Say That I Am? Christians Encounter Other Religions* (Scottdale, Pa.: Herald Press, 1997), 24.

11. Ibid., 24.

12. Ulanov, *Wisdom of the Psyche,* 109.

13. Ibid., 110.

14. Ibid., 111.

15. Ibid., 113.

16. Ibid., 117.

17. Shenk, *Who Do You Say That I Am?* 62.

18. Ibid., 132.

19. Ibid. Jesus explains to his followers that they cannot know who he is unless God reveals this truth to them: Matthew 16:15-17. See also Matthew 11:25-27; John 16:7-15.

20. Ibid., 74.

21. Tilden Edwards, *Sabbath Time: Understanding and Practice for Contemporary Christians,* rev. ed. (Nashville: Upper Room Books, 2003), 16.

22. Ibid.

23. Ruffing, *Uncovering Stories of Faith,* 55.

## CHAPTER 3

1. See Luke 15. See also chapter 1 for my reference to "honkings."

2. George R. Brunk III, "In the Beginning Is the End," unpublished convocation message given at Eastern Mennonite Seminary, August 26, 1998. Brunk pays attention to the relationship between our own stories and the gospel story in which our lives are imbedded and thus he invites our attention to Luke's concern for the individual and how each individual finds purpose and meaning in the context of the gospel story.

3. Ulrich Simon, *Story and Faith in the Biblical Narrative* (London: SPCK, 1975), ix, 17.

4. I am indebted to Dr. Joseph Maclatchey for this holistic overview concerning all stories telling the same story. He was professor of English literature at Wheaton College and offered it during his opening comments to a course in creative writing.

5. Luke records this shift from the old story to the new in the lives of two disciples in his narrative of the Emmaus journey. See Luke 24.

6. Luke 1:1, 2; John 20:30, 31. See also Acts 1:1-3. George R. Brunk III points to this scholarly and pastoral dimension of Luke's literary work, thus implying that this work of noticing God's presence and work as well as the task of paying attention to our responses to God are part of the work of pastoral ministry.

7. See Guenther, *Holy Listening,* 32: "The director's task is to help connect the individual's story to the story and thereby help the directee to recognize and claim identity in Christ, discern the action of the Holy Spirit. There is a God-component in all human experience, even in lives that seem pain-filled and remote from God. A sense of God's absence or remorse at one's own inattentiveness to God's presence can be a fruitful place for beginning direction."

8. "Explanation of General Format," New American Standard Bible (Carol Stream, Ill.: Creation House, 1972), x.

9. Ibid.

10. G. L. Phillips quoted in *The Anchor Bible* (Garden City, NY: Doubleday & Company, Inc., 1966), 502.

11. I am indebted to John Koenig's scholarly and contemplative insight here.

12. Wendy Miller, *Invitation to Presence: A Guide to Spiritual Disciplines* (Nashville, Tenn.: Upper Room Books, 1995), 81. See also Richard Foster in *Celebration of Discipline: The Path to Spiritual Growth,* rev. ed. (San Francisco: HarperSanFrancisco, 1988), Chapter 2, "Meditation."

13. Jack Dean Kingsbury, *Matthew as Story,* 19.

14. Miller, *Invitation to Presence,* 51. See also Simon Tugwell's helpful insights into what is meant within the Hebrew understanding of the term *heart:* "A modern reader is liable to misunderstand this, because for him 'heart' will almost certainly suggest 'the seat of the emotions', contrasted, as likely as not, with 'head', taken to be the seat of thought. But the ancient world, whether we are thinking of Semitic peoples or Greeks and Romans, made different connexions between parts of the body and psychological functions. The Hebrews allocated different emotions to different parts of the body, but not to the heart in particular. . . . The heart was taken more generally to stand for the 'inner man', and in particular for the mind and the will. . . . [Heart] does not, then, refer to the heart as the seat of the emotions, but to the whole interiority of human consciousness and activity. The heart is a symbol of what we are in ourselves, of the source of all our reactions and aspirations." *The Beatitudes: Soundings in Christian Traditions* (Springfield, Ill.: Templegate Publishers, 1980), 94.

15. Ruthellen Josselson, "Imagining the Real: Empathy, Narrative, and the Dialogic Self" in Ruthellen Josselson and Anna Lieblich, eds., *Interpreting Experience: The Narrative Study of Lives,* vol. 3 (Thousand Oaks, Calif.: Sage Publications, 1995), 31.

16. Susan E. Chase, "Taking Narrative Seriously: Consequences for Method and Theory in Interview Studies" in Josselson and Lieblich, *Interpreting Experience,* 2.

## CHAPTER 4

1. Calvin J. Roetzel, *The World That Shaped the New Testament* (Atlanta, Ga.: John Knox Press, 1985), 16, 17.

## CHAPTER 5

1. David Rensberger, "Deserted Spaces," *Weavings* 16, no. 3 (May/June 2001), 7–13. In his reflection, Rensberger draws attention to the word used in Greek which is commonly translated "desert" or "wilderness": *erémos*. "It means uninhabited, lonely, with no human population. The *erémos* is a *desolate* location, whatever may be the reason for its desolation. . . . Indeed, precisely because it is empty of the distractions that are encountered in civilized places, and above all empty of occasions to demonstrate one's prowess or wisdom or brilliance to other people, the uninhabited land offers a rich setting for developing the depths of the spirit's capacities. . . . We *will* be tested to find out if there is anything we love more than God. Our lives . . . are at God's disposal now, and are subject to rearrangement in ways we may not at all anticipate or desire."

2. The Herodians are a group loyal to the political and personal interests of Herod Antipas, ruler of Galilee at the time of Jesus. Although this is an unlikely allegiance, the Pharisees and the Herodians find a common ground in their opposition to Jesus and his teaching.

3. Mary Ann Scofield, "Friends of God and Prophets: 2002 SDI Symposium Address" in *Presence: The Journal of Spiritual Directors International* 8, no. 3 (October, 2002): 37.

## CHAPTER 6

1. Hans Denck, "The Contention that Scripture Says," 1526, in *Anabaptism in Outline,* ed. Walter Klassen (Scottdale, Pa.: Herald Press, 1981), 48.

2. Gerald May, *Will and Spirit: A Contemplative Psychology* (San Francisco: HarperSanFrancisco, 1982), 92.

3. Contents of this paragraph were included in "Spiritual Formation," an article written by the author and published in *Lectionary Homiletics* 9, no. 3 (February 1998): 8.

## CHAPTER 7

1. *The Rule of St. Benedict in English,* ed. Timothy Fry (Collegeville, Minn.: The Liturgical Press, 1982), 15, 16.

2. Ibid., 28.

3. See again Simon Tugwell's valuable insight regarding the concept of *heart* in the scripture as quoted in note 14 of chapter 3.

4. From a conversation among Abba Moses, John Cassian, and Germanus, in *John Cassian: The Conferences,* trans. Boniface Ramsey (New York: Paulist Press, 1997), 63.

5. Walter Brueggemann, *Praying the Psalms* (Winona, Minn.: St. Mary's Press, 1993),14, 18–19.

## CHAPTER 8

1. Bernard of Clairvaux in "On Consideration," in *The Very Thought of Thee: From Three Great Mystics: Bernard of Clairvaux, Jeremy Taylor, Evelyn Underhill,* arr. and ed. by Douglas V. Steere and J. Minton Batten (Nashville, Tenn.: The Upper Room, 1953), 14–15.

2. Brueggemann, *Praying the Psalms,* 18–19. See also Psalm 13 in which "How long?" is repeated as an integral part of this prayer of lament.

3. John Koenig, *New Testament Hospitality* (Eugene, Ore.: Wipf and Stock Publishers, 2001), 15–16.

## CHAPTER 9

1. Thomas R. Kelly, *A Testament of Devotion* (New York: Harper & Brothers Publishers, 1941), 35.

2. Ibid.

3. Saint Teresa of Avila, *The Collected Works of St. Teresa of Avila,* vol. 2, trans. Kieran Kavanaugh and Otilio Rodriguez (Washington, D.C.: ICS Publications, 1980), 284, 286.

4. Evagrius Ponticus, *The Prakticos and Chapters on Prayer,* trans. by John E. Bamberger (Kalamazoo, Mich.: Cistercian Publications, 1981), 17.

## CHAPTER 10

1. Chaim Potok, *My Name is Asher Lev* (New York: Ballantine Books, 1996), 170.

2. John Cassian, *John Cassian: The Conferences,* "Seventh Conference: On the Soul and Evil Spirits," trans. Boniface Ramsey (New York: Paulist Press, 1997) III.3, 248-49.

3. Ibid., IV.3, 250.

4. William Johnston, ed., *The Cloud of Unknowing* (New York: Image Books, Doubleday, 1973), 48–49.

5. Alvarez de Paz, cited in Kenneth Leech, *Soul Friend: The Practice of Christian Spirituality* (San Francisco: Harper & Row, 1977), 129.

6. The Book of Common Prayer (New York: Oxford University Press, 1999), 219.

## CHAPTER 11

1. John's account of Mary's anointing Jesus focuses only on Judas Iscariot's critical reaction and does not mention how the other disciples respond. However, I am assuming they were just as angry and scolding in their reaction toward Mary because in other accounts of similar anointings, those present expressed anger and rejection. In Mark 14:5, "they scolded her." Matthew 26:6-13 specifically mentions the other disciples' negative retort. For a laborer in Jesus' time, three hundred denarii would equal nearly a year's wages.

2. Footnote reading in Matthew 26:28.

## CHAPTER 12

1. Sandra Cronk, *Dark Night Journey: Inward Re-patterning Toward a Life Centered in God* (Wallingford, Pa.: Pendle Hill Publications, 1991), 38.

2. John of the Cross, "The Dark Night" Book II.5.4 in *The Collected Works of St. John of the Cross*, trans. Kieran Kavanaugh and Otilio Rodriguez (Washington, D.C.: ICS Publications, 1979), 336.

3. Cornelius J. Dyck, ed., *Spiritual Life in Anabaptism* (Scottdale, Pa.: Herald Press, 1995), 194.

4. Ibid., 195, 196. Hans Schlaffer and the other Anabaptist believers were executed in February 1528.

5. Hippolytus of Rome, "The Times for Prayer," in "The Apostolic Tradition of Hippolytus of Rome," in Lucien Deiss, *Springtime of the Liturgy: Liturgical Texts of the First Four Centuries,* trans. Matthew J. O'Connell (Collegeville, Minn.: The Liturgical Press, 1979), 151.

6. Ibid.

7. Ibid., 151–52.

## CHAPTER 13

1. Ulanov, *The Wisdom of the Psyche,* 46, 47.

2. Bernard of Clairvaux, "On Loving God" in *The Very Thought of Thee,* ed. Douglas V. Steere and J. Minton Batten, 23.

# ABOUT THE AUTHOR

WENDY MILLER is campus pastor and assistant professor of spiritual formation at Eastern Mennonite Seminary in Harrisonburg, Virginia, where she also directs the Summer Institute for Spiritual Formation. A graduate of Iowa Wesleyan College, she earned a master's degree in church leadership at Eastern Mennonite Seminary and a master's degree in sacred theology at General Theological Seminary in New York.